The Lawbook Exchange, Ltd.

## Foundations of the
## American Law of Lawyering
## Series

GENERAL EDITOR
Michael H. Hoeflich
*John H. & John M. Kane Professor of Law*
*University of Kansas School of Law*

# The Ethics of Compensation
# for Professional Services

*An Address Before the Albany Law School
and an Answer to Hostile Critiques*

# Foundations of the
# American Law of Lawyering

The Foundations of the American Law of Lawyering Series presents reprints of works published in the nineteenth and early twentieth century that illuminate the ethical origins of the heritage of the legal profession in the United States.

## TITLES IN THE SERIES

**The Ethics of Compensation for Professional Services**
An Address Before the Albany Law School and an Answer to Hostile Critiques
Edwin Countryman

**Sources of the History of the American Law of Lawyering**
Michael H. Hoeflich, Editor

**"You Should Not."**
A Book for Lawyers, Old and Young, Containing the Elements of Legal Ethics
Samuel H. Wandell

# THE

# Ethics of Compensation

FOR

## PROFESSIONAL SERVICES:

## AN ADDRESS

BEFORE

## THE ALBANY LAW SCHOOL

AND AN

## ANSWER TO HOSTILE CRITIQUES.

BY

## EDWIN COUNTRYMAN.

With a new introduction by
Michael H. Hoeflich
*University of Kansas School of Law*

THE LAWBOOK EXCHANGE, LTD.
Clark, New Jersey

ISBN 978-1-61619-474-1

Lawbook Exchange edition 2017

*The quality of this reprint is equivalent to the quality of the original work.*

THE LAWBOOK EXCHANGE, LTD.
33 Terminal Avenue
Clark, New Jersey 07066-1321

*Please see our website for a selection of our other publications
and fine facsimile reprints of classic works of legal history:*
www.lawbookexchange.com

**Library of Congress Cataloging-in-Publication Data**

Names: Countryman, Edwin, 1833-1914, author. | Hoeflich, Michael
   H., writer of introduction.
Title: The ethics of compensation for professional services : an address
   before the albany law school and an answer to hostile critiques / by
   Edwin  Countryman ; with a new introduction by Michael H.
   Hoeflich, John H. and  John M. Kane Professor of Law, University of
   Kansas School of Law.
Description: Lawbook Exchange edition. | Clark, NJ : The Lawbook
   Exchange,  Ltd., 2016. | Series: Foundations of the American law of
   lawyering |
   Includes index.
Identifiers: LCCN 2016050872 | ISBN 9781616194741 (hardcover : alk.
   paper)
Subjects: LCSH: Contingent fees--United States. | Lawyers--Fees--
   United States.
Classification: LCC KF310.C6 C68 2016 | DDC 344.7301/28134--dc23
LC record available at https://lccn.loc.gov/2016050872

*Printed in the United States of America on acid-free paper*

# INTRODUCTION

Michael H. Hoeflich

Judge Edwin Countryman's *The Ethics of Compensation for Professional Services* began life as an address to the student body of Albany Law School. One may imagine that Judge Countryman, who was anything but a radical, probably assumed that his speech would not attract national attention nor have lasting impact on the practice of the American Bar. But Irving Browne, a prominent Albany lawyer, author and editor of the *Albany Law Review*, was apparently so outraged by Judge Countryman's remarks that he not only dedicated space in his periodical to a severe critique of these remarks, but sought out the negative opinions on Judge Countryman's remarks of several leading lights of the contemporary American Bar including Justice Bradley of the United States Supreme Court. What brought on such a massive response to an Upstate New York judge's remarks to a class of law students? In short, Judge Countryman's address made the case for permitting lawyers to utilize contingent fee arrangements.

Contingent fees have been controversial in the Anglo-American legal tradition for centuries. Generally, a contingent fee is a fee that is payable only if a lawsuit is successful and one which is generally expressed as a percentage of value of any recovery that is due to the client upon the successful conclusion of the suit. Essential to the notion of a contingent fee is risk, the risk that the lawyer will receive no fee unless his client wins. Stanford Law

School Professor Janet Cooper Alexander has defined a contingency fee in these terms:

> In its pure form, the contingent fee is a pre-filing contractual agreement setting the attorney's fee as a percentage of the recovery... If no recovery is obtained, the attorney receives no fee. Contingent fee agreements can be viewed as a form of non-recourse, secured financing agreement; as a commission agreement; or as a partnership or joint venture in which the client contributes the claim and the lawyer contributes the expertise and the effort necessary to realize the claim.[1]

The perception that contingent fees are problematic ethically goes back to some early Common law doctrines: champerty, barratry, and maintenance, doctrines that prohibited the sale and purchase of legal cases. These doctrines developed because there arose in Medieval England a practice in which a wealthy nobleman would purchase a claim, often an extremely weak claim, from someone with less power to pursue it, then litigate the claim in court and exercise extrajudicial influence [through the nobleman's political, financial, and military power] to ensure that he was successful. In effect, these doctrines were developed to combat a particularly insidious form of abuse of the common law courts. Although contingent fee arrangements rarely involved the types of abuse present in these medieval suits, the traditional fear of these was so great that English judges and legislators extended the

---

[1] J.C. Alexander, "Contingent Fees and Class Actions,"*De Paul Law Review*. vol. 47 (1997), pp. 397 ff.

medieval doctrines of champerty, barratry, and maintenance to prohibit contingent fees as a whole.[2]

In the United States, there was far less concern for the types of abuses associated with contingent fees in England and the advantages of contingent fee arrangements were much more widely appreciated. Lawyers, judges, and legislators in nineteenth century America realized that contingent fee arrangements generally increased access to the courts for those people who did not have the financial means to afford to pay either a flat fee or an hourly fee, both of which generally required up front and/or interim payments. Professor Karsten, in his classic article, "Enabling the Poor to Have Their Day in Court: The Sanctioning if Contingency Fee Contracts, A History to 1940" demonstrates that contingent fee contracts were widely used in the United States throughout much of the nineteenth century.[3]

By the late nineteenth century the nature of the American Bar had changed along with the structure of the American economy. After the Civil War, American industry changed from one comprised primarily of small businesses served by general practitioners alone or in small firms to an industry that was increasingly concentrated, in which the great railroad, steel, and oil corporations had become dominant and which were served by the new "corporate lawyers" who worked in large firms dedicated to serving these large, complex industrial enterprises.[4] One of the greatest dangers to these new corporations, particularly the railroads, was the rising tide of personal injury suits brought

---

[2] For a recent American discussion of these doctrines, see, Osprey, Inc. *v.* Cabana Ltd. P'ship, 532 S.E.2d 269, 273 (S.C. 2000) (quoting In re Primus, 436 U.S. 412, 424 n.15 (1978)).

[3] P. Karsten, "Enabling the Poor to Have Their Day in Court...," *De Paul Law Review*, vol. 47 (1997), pp. 231ff.

[4] See, M.H.Hoeflich, S. Wandel, *You Should Not* (2014) at 7.

by workers and by passengers injured in industrial accidents. One response by these corporations and the lawyers who served them to defend these suits, often brought by plaintiffs with few financial resources, was to lobby for ethical rules that prohibited contingent fee arrangements or any fee arrangements that expanded access to the courts beyond the favored few. The purpose, of course, was to prevent most, of these annoying (to the corporate defendants) plaintiffs from bringing their suits. It was at the same time as this movement to prohibit contingent fee financing was gaining ground in the United States that a second movement, to begin to regulate lawyer behavior through formal codes of professional responsibility, was gaining ground.[5] The effect of this was that many of the ethics codes of the late nineteenth and early twentieth century incorporated strict ethical prohibitions against the use of contingent fee arrangements by lawyers.

Certainly, all of the parties to the debate centered around Judge Countryman's remarks were aware that such fees were in daily use. To understand the debate, it is useful to also understand the lives and personalities of those involved.

Judge Edwin Countryman was born in Fort Plain, New York in 1833, but moved to Cherry Valley, N.Y. when young.[6] He was admitted to the New York Bar in 1854 and

---

[5] See, C. Andrews, "Standards of Conduct for Lawyers: An 800 Year Evolution," *SMU Law Review*, vol. 57 (2004), pp. 1434ff.; P. M. Pruitt, Jr., "Thomas Goode Jones: Personal Code of a Public Man," in *Gilded Age Legal Ethics: Essays on Thomas Goode Jones' 1887 Code*(2003).
[6] Biographical details are drawn from *Proceedings of the Annual Meeting of the New York Bar Association Annual Meeting* (1915), pp. 818–821.

entered private practice. Early in his career he entered into a partnership with Nathaniel C. Moak, who was himself to go to prominence at the New York Bar.[7]

In 1860 Countryman was elected as District Attorney of Otsego County. During his term, he moved to Cooperstown, the County seat of Otsego County. In 1867 he was appointed the Register in Bankruptcy for the Nineteenth Congressional District and was also appointed a justice of the Supreme Court of New York for the Sixth Judicial District, an office which he held only for a short time, leaving the bench in 1874. In 1876 Countryman moved to Albany and remained in private practice there until his death. He had a number of partners during this period, including Judge Amasa Parker. His practice would appear to have been lucrative. When he died in 1915 he left an estate valued at $225,000, a substantial sum for the period.

Judge Countryman was not content simply with the practice of law and public service. He was also an author of legal scholarship including a book on the United States Supreme Court.[8] Thus, his choice as a speaker at the Albany Law School was hardly unusual. The reaction to that speech, however, was.

Of all the many lawyers and law students in the audience who heard Judge Countryman's speech in 1881, none was more important—nor more engaged with it and outraged by it—than Irving Browne.

Irving Browne was born in Oneida County, N.Y. in 1835 to a Universalist pastor and his wife.[9] The family

---

[7] See, "Nathaniel C. Moak," *Cornell Law Jl.*, v. 1 (1894), pp.94–.

[8] See, Edwin Countryman, *The Supreme Court of the United States: with a review of certain decisions relating to its appellate power under the Constitution* (1913).

[9] Biographical details are drawn from *History of Rensselaer County, New York,* online at www.rootsweb.ancestry.com/-nyrensse/bio22.htm; and from the website *Strangers to Us All* online at myweb.wvnet.edu/-jelkins/lp-2001/browne.html.

moved around when he was a child so that he lived in New York, Connecticut, and New Hampshire. He read law in the office of Judge Theodore Miller in Hudson, N.Y. and studied at Albany Law School from 1856 to 1857 when he graduated. He practiced law in New York City, and Troy, N.Y. until 1879 when he moved to New York to become the editor of the *Albany Law Journal*. At the time he assumed the editorship the *Albany Law Journal* was one of the leading legal periodicals in the Unites States.[10] He also became the editor of the *American Law Reports* at the same time. These two positions gave Browne an unchallenged bully pulpit from which to propound his ideas to the American legal profession. In addition to his editorial duties, Browne was a prolific author of poetry, prose, and legal scholarship. He also served as a lecturer at the Albany Law School. He died in 1899.

Thus, it is quite clear that Irving Browne would have been a formidable opponent in any legal or literary controversy. That he took such umbrage to Judge Countryman's remarks is, however, somewhat surprising. Browne was certainly not a conventional Upstate New York lawyer. He was an author, a literateur, and a book collector of note. Certainly, one would not expect him to have held either liberal or radical political and professional opinions, but, the vehemence with which he attacked Judge Countryman's remarks suggests a passionate opposition, one far beyond the norm.

Essentially, Browne was a member of the legal elite. His magazine catered to the legal elite, those lawyers who had the time and finances to read not only reports but the scholarly articles the *Albany Law Journal* published. Unlike the common run of the bar, Browne loved literature and

---

[10] See, M.H. Hoeflich, "Legal Periodicals," in S. Stern & Nan Goodman, *Law & Humanities in Nineteenth Century America* (2017).

books and wrote poetry. These are the activities of an elite lawyer. And, as noted above, the elite of the American Bar at the end of the nineteenth century was almost unanimously opposed to contingent fee arrangements precisely because they widened access to the court system to the unwashed and penurious multitudes who could only obtain legal address for their injuries on a contingent basis. It also opposed those who brought these suits, in many cases minority lawyers and immigrants or sons and daughters of immigrants and minority lawyers who did not fit the elite image of a white Anglo-Saxon profession. Judge Countryman's remarks must have seemed tantamount to "class treason" to Browne and those from whom he sought support.

Particular insight into the importance of this controversy may be gained from looking at a short review of Judge Countryman's published remarks that appeared in the eighth volume of the Pacific Coast Law Journal.[11] The reviewer was obviously intrigued by the vitriol of the arguments between Judge Countryman and Irving Browne and, perhaps, a bit surprised at the arguments at all. The reviewer characterized Judge Countryman's remarks as "stirring up a hornet's nest." He also characterizes Judge Countryman's published response to the opinions of Judges Cooley and Dillon and Justice Bradley as "very forcible specimen[s] of the argument *ad hominem.*" Yet, for all the reviewer's surprise at the sharpness of the exchange, on the actual subject of the debate, whether contingent fees should be deemed to be unethical and impermissible for lawyer-client compensation arrangements, the reviewer takes a moderate, even pragmatic position:

---

[11] "Compensation for Legal Services," *Pacific Coast Law Journal*, vol. 8 (1881-82), pp.836–837.

Clients and attorneys will regulate this matter to suit themselves. If the old common law, with its old ideas in this regard, stands in the way, the statute will supersede it, and leave this question to be settled upon business principles, with no restraints but that of honesty.[12]

In time, Judge Countryman's ideas about contingent fees came to be accepted much as the anonymous reviewer in the *Pacific Coast Law Journal* predicted. By the end of World War II many lawyers and legislators were coming to realize that the benefits of contingent fee financing and other creative, non-traditional financing arrangements outweighed any problems that they might cause. As a result, the ethics codes of the postwar era began to loosen up the restrictions on contingent fee and other non-traditional financing arrangements, a trend that continues to this day. There is still some concern among lawyers and disciplinary authorities for possible abuses that may occur in the use of contingent fee arrangements, but, generally, if in most cases certain safeguards are observed, contingent fees are permitted. In a few areas, including domestic arrangements, contingent fees are still prohibited. But these are limited cases today. Thus, Judge Countryman's late nineteenth century defense of contingent fee arrangements stands as an early and influential argument for a fee arrangement that has become both permissible and common.

---

[12] Ibid., at p. 837.

THE

# Ethics of Compensation

FOR

## PROFESSIONAL SERVICES:

### AN ADDRESS

BEFORE

# THE ALBANY LAW SCHOOL

AND AN

## ANSWER TO HOSTILE CRITIQUES.

BY

EDWIN COUNTRYMAN.

ALBANY:
W. C. LITTLE & CO., LAW BOOK PUBLISHERS.
1882.

Geonge C. Riggs, Printer, Stereotyper and Binder,
461 Broadway, Albany, N. Y.

" There is a great deal of false sentiment in the world on the subject of lawyer's fees. * * In some extra-sentimental communities lawyers are forbidden to demand any compensation, and are left to the mercy of those whom they serve. In very many communities lawyers are prohibited from having any pecuniary interest in the result of the suits in which they are employed. * * All these ideas are remnants of a system which in most other respects we have outgrown. They are founded in the same belief in total depravity which for so many centuries denied to an accused person the privilege of being sworn in his own behalf. * * We do not agree with some that it is reprehensible in a lawyer to have an interest in the possible recovery for his compensation. There is probably not a layman in the country who would think it indelicate or oppressive in his lawyer to decline to demand compensation in a case where his client was defeated, or to estimate his compensation upon a per centage of the recovery in a case where he was successful. Indeed it is the constant practice of lawyers to mitigate their charges where their clients have not proved successful, and to share in their success. Now, what is the objection to making the arrangement a matter of pre-contract?"

13 *Albany Law Journal*, 379–380.

" Lawyers and suitors must be left to deal with each other like other persons of common sense and ordinary experience. Suitors will occasionally be fleeced by dishonest lawyers, but where one such case occurs, nineteen lawyers will be cheated by dishonest clients. There is a great deal too much of this sentimental nonsense in regard to the members of the learned professions. A physician must not advertise; a clergyman must not care for the amount of his salary; a lawyer must not have any pecuniary interest in the result of his client's cause. We had supposed that the sturdy sense of our profession had weeded out this last idea. We knew it was legally extinct, we hoped it was morally defunct."

10 *Albany Law Journal*, 194.

"There are very many just causes of action to which the courts ought to devote their attention, and which are only prevented from being brought before them by the pecuniary disabilities of worthy would-be suitors. And in such a case the encouragement of a friend, be he attorney or layman, is a very proper means of helping along a worthy client in a worthy cause, in the proceeds of which neither public policy, morality nor common justice would declare that his supporter should not share."

6 *Albany Law Journal*, 136.

# PREFACE.

A preface to an occasional address needs an explanation. The editor of the Albany Law Journal who was present as one of the faculty when the address was delivered, was moved to make in his journal of the following week a rude attack upon the author as the disseminator of dangerous doctrines among the graduates. The particular topic that excited his choler was that relating to contingent fees for the services of advocacy. Although the Law Journal had been in former years a sturdy defender of the same view, the editor affected to believe that this was the first time the propriety of an agreement between attorney and client for contingent remuneration had been publicly maintained. Amazed at the publication of a dictum so preposterous, a brief note was addressed to the editor, calling his attention to several authorities where the proposition had been adjudicated. These authorities instead of allaying apparently increased the editorial irritation. He replied with a budget of choice excerpts, which, though mainly irrelevant, were greatly prized by him because they contained bitter denunciations of professional practices that could be readily perverted and pointed against "the adversary." A rejoinder followed, to which was added a postscript containing extracts from the Law Journal, fully sustaining the doctrines of the address; but this postscript, it is needful to state, the editor categorically refused to publish! All of these articles, however, are now subjoined in the appendix, together with the rejected postscript.

The fastidious editor continued for several weeks a scattering fire against the "ignoble views" contained in the address. Evidently dissatisfied with the state of the authorities on the subject, he resorted to several equivocal expedients to overcome the difficulty. While declining to allow his readers to see his deceased predecessor's authentic "apology" of a practice so "pernicious," his highly conservative moral tone, (which he is frank to state has been largely acquired since he left the bar,) did not restrain him from attempting a "pious fraud" upon the memory of a departed friend, by a post-mortem accusation of his repentance and retraction of earnest living utterances! By adopting this effective mode, (à la Madame Littré) of dealing with the literary remains of an "advanced thinker," the editor evinced perhaps a pardonable desire to weaken the weight of wicked opinions, while he silenced the most annoying of opposing authorities, and upheld the oracular consistency of his journal.

But his controversial resources were not exhausted by this summary excision of offensive quotations. He developed a rare capacity for extemporizing measures to propagate precepts and precedents for any emergency. If there were, indeed, no judicial authorities favoring his views, he was clear in conscience that there ought to be, and he would improvise them accordingly. His devices to attain this purpose were as novel as they were effective and opportune. He selected his own judges, submitted to them privately an ex-parte statement of the controversy, with such collateral suggestions as were doubtless adapted to inspire the strictest impartiality, and actually obtained several *ex-cathedrà* opinions for publication in his journal! Nor was there any lack of his usual discrimination in the composition of his special commission. The tact and assurance of the editor and the delicacy displayed by the distinguished gentlemen in accepting their allotted positions, are alike worthy of particular note. Two of them, the Law Journal states, are acting judges high in authority, and two of them are likewise "lecturers at law schools;" and all of them "represent the purest morals and highest intellect in our profession."

It is also fair to presume, considering the criticisms made upon Webster and Bayard, that none of these select gentlemen ever held "slaves" or "thought it right" to do so, while all of them may be "credited with the very finest feelings about money matters." Still it may not be inappropriate under the circumstances to ascertain their special qualifications for the duties they have so punctiliously assumed.

The editor takes particular pleasure in stating that two of them, like himself, are "lecturers at law schools." But really, is this vocation, in these latter days, the highest recommendation—is it, in view of the peculiar practices charged upon some of these institutions, specially adapted to develope and sharpen the ethical rather than the commercial faculties? Does the fact that a professor shares in a speculation by which hundreds of youth are annually yerked into the legal profession in violation of established rules, at a regular rate *per capita*, enable him to "speak as one having authority," of the mercenary motives of his brethren at the bar? Does his rare experience and good fortune in profiting by the labors of his students, who are permitted to pass precious portions of their short novitiates in the purlieus of the Legislature, lobbying for laws to enable the faculty to circumvent the courts, tend

to clarify his conscience, enlarge his moral acumen
and qualify him above all others to critically weigh
and determine questions of professional ethics?
Doubtless the editor, whose thriving career at the
bar entitles him to jeer at Daniel Webster "about
money matters," and whose erratic conscience
changes so conveniently with every varying interest
of his life that a practice which seemed harmless
enough when he was trying to make a little money
by it,* now appears from his professorial chair so
"pernicious," that he is utterly "disheartened" at

---

\* The editor states his own position in the Law Journal thus:
"The difference between Judge C. and ourselves on this sub‑
ject is right here; we would take just as few cases of this
kind as possible, he would get just as many of them as he could.
We would publish our strong reluctance and disapprobation, he
would advertise his approval and readiness to be persuaded." Dis‑
avowing his impertinent assumption to speak for others, I concede
the right of the editor to represent his own views. But then he
is under some obligation to state his position with accuracy and
precision. Does he refer to himself in the above extract as an
editor or practitioner? If the former, the assertion is excessively
cheap for one who has abandoned the profession. But if he refers
to his practice while at the bar, his statement suggests and tenders
a material issue which I accept. I am informed by those having
the best opportunities of knowledge, that so long as he remained in
practice, the editor "advertised his readiness" to accept contin‑
gent retainers, and "got just as many of them as he could."
Lest, however, there may be ground for misapprehension, I offer
to refer the issue to three of his professional brethren—one from
each of the leading law firms in the city of Troy, where he lived
at the time—to be selected by himself. I only stipulate for notice
of the hearing, and the right to offer countervailing evidence.

the bare suggestion of its propriety to a class of
graduates—without a question the ingenuous professor conceives that he can now appreciate "this
matter in its real moral bearings better than he
could" before, and therefore naturally infers that
others having the same diversified experiences must
necessarily possess the highest qualifications for the
duties of his modern areopagus. And yet the profession at large, bearing in mind the "mischievous
seeds" they have sown and the baneful results to
the bar of their money making achievements during
the last thirty years, may deem it quite expedient,
not to yield unreservedly to the arrogant assumptions of these ambitious "lecturers at law schools."

But these unobtrusive gentlemen have enjoyed
other marked advantages specially fitting them for
their designated duties, which did not escape the
wary editor and cannot be permitted to pass unno-
ticed. One of them is reputed to have made his
fortune at the bar as a corporation attorney ; and
he signalized his elevation to the bench by promptly
assisting to overrule the deliberate decision of that
high tribunal, adverse to corporate interests, on a
great and vital question of public policy. Another,
directly on retiring from the bench, entered the
professional arena as a leading champion of corporate concerns, and is now almost exclusively engaged

in representing these institutions in the courts. The third has long been noted for his judicial tendencies toward restricting the liability of corporations to the narrowest limit. It is quite within the range of moderation to state that no judge in this country has gone further, as a rule, in exempting corporations from legal accountability for injuries caused by their fault or· negligence to others. These remarks are not made in a spirit of censure or criticism, but merely to indicate the natural and even necessary attitude of these gentlemen on the subject of debate. It will appear in the sequel how corporate interests and influences may bias the opinions of men on a question of this character.

The solicitude of the editor to secure an impartial arbitrament is also evident from another important circumstance. One of his selections is made from the only State in which the theory of the honorarium has been approved by the courts.* Of course an advocate, taught to believe that any preliminary contract for his services was undignified and immoral, and who had always practiced by the proverb that "a bird in the hand is worth two in the bush,"

---

* Seeley v. Crane, 15 N. J. Law, 35; Van Atta v. McKinney's Exrs., 16 N. J. Law, 235; Schomp v. Schenck, 40 N. J. Law, 195, 197, 200

could not hesitate to condemn a contingent fee ; and the astute editor was as safe in choosing him to sit in his commission as he would have been with an English barrister, or Chief Justice HOBART himself. Another selection was clearly controlled by the same discreet and discerning motive. The Supreme Court of Michigan is the only American tribunal upholding agreements for professional services, which has gone the length of pronouncing a contract for a contingent fee to be *malum in se.*\* And the Michigan member of the commission was rightly supposed to be too conservative and constant to abandon the doctrines of his own tribunal.

Waiving, however, these precursory considerations which, after all, are important merely to exhibit the adroitness of the editor in maneuvering to secure unbiased arbiters and to obtain an impartial decision against his opponent, to herald to the profession in his journal, I proceed to examine the merits of the controversy. Dropping personal topics, I pass into the realm of principles, and purpose to review the arguments of my reviewers. If the reasons given for their conclusions be incontestable,

---

\* Backus *v.* Byron, 4 Mich., 535. Happily, however, in 1867, the Legislature overruled the court, and attorneys are now "allowed to make such agreements for compensation as they see fit." Wells *v.* Elsam, 40 Mich., 220.

it is of little moment whether they were prejudiced and partial, or their methods of disputation were in plain violation of the rules of legitimate warfare. And if their reasoning be found to be inconsequential, I have little fear that their professional prestige or judicial authority will suffice to overthrow the conclusions of common sense, or the decisive tests of the collective experience of the bar.

As there was presumably no preliminary interchange of views, and the opinions were delivered separately, it was quite natural to anticipate some diversity in the reasons assigned for the same general conclusion. But the members of this tribunal must have been amused, if not amazed, when they came to read their deliverances collectively in the Law Journal. Their methods of reaching the same result are so dissimilar and discordant that the arguments of one are answered by the admissions and assumptions of the others. It would suffice, on the essential points, to place in juxtaposition the leading propositions of their "opinions," using each in turn to controvert and confute the others. A brief general survey of their positions will make this apparent.

Mr. Justice BRADLEY is content with a dogmatic statement of his views, based on the assumption that the English law of champerty is controlling and conclusive. He is pertinaciously opposed to *any* preliminary agreement for professional remuneration; but, after the service has been performed, he sees "no harm in *asking* for a fee proportioned to the degree of success," or receiving in payment a portion of the property recovered. Ex-Judge DILLON naively confesses—for he is clearly alluding to his own experience—that "*most* professional charges are *sub modo* contingent; that is, a lawyer charges more for the same skill and labor where they lead to a successful result than where they do not." But the key-note of Mr. Justice COOLEY'S argument is contained in the proposition that "the lawyer's legitimate fee is payable irrespective of the result;" and that *any* contingent interest in the event of the litigation is necessarily "corrupting," so that it "affects injuriously all his professional relations." The leading thought, therefore, of the latter, which he has carefully elaborated as the principal objection to contingent fees, is tacitly assumed by both of his associates to be untenable—indeed, both of them distinctly intimate their approval of the practice of receiving fees "proportioned to the degree of success," provided there is no formal agreement, or "expression," as ex-Judge DILLON would term it, to that effect.

With the majority, then, the issue is reduced to

a very narrow compass. The impropriety of contingent compensation depends upon the fact of an "express" agreement. The retainer may be accepted, and the service rendered, with the *expectation* on the part of the attorney of receiving a contingent fee, which he must be careful not to "express" to the client or reduce to the form of a contract. But after the case is closed he may charge, or retain out of the proceeds in his hands, a fee proportioned to the result. He must be governed, however, solely by his own judgment in determining the amount, as it is beneath his dignity to "dicker" with his client on such a sordid and trivial subject. By pursuing this course he will be respected and regarded by all "high minded" lawyers as "regular" in his professional practices. But if he is so imprudent as to entertain negotiations beforehand, and enter into a fair arrangement with his client to accept precisely the same terms for the service, and honorably performs the agreement, he will, in the judgment of the majority of this extraordinary tribunal, be guilty of an act "derogatory to the honor of the profession!"

Upon what principle of ethics, I pause to inquire, is it dishonorable to obtain the consent of the client to your doing that which it is right to do, with or without his consent, when the contingency has occurred? Upon what recondite rule of reason do these subtle casuists rely for their assumption, that it is wrong to make a preliminary contract for a fee "proportioned to the degree of success," but perfectly proper to ask for and secure such a fee after success has been attained? Why is it improper to express in terms the expectation of the parties, or the implication which the law supplies from their acts and proceedings? It is a legal presumption that a party has agreed to pay for accepted services what, under all the circumstances, he ought to pay. This presumption is founded on the rule of equity, that it is only just a person should make due return for a benefit received. The law, therefore, in the absence of any express arrangement, implies a promise to this effect and enforces payment accordingly.* Is it immoral, then, to declare explicitly beforehand what the law will subsequently infer and imply from the acts of the parties? Is not this rather ingenious theory a curious inversion of the rule, equally familiar in law and morals, that a man may not do indirectly what he cannot do directly?

Judge BRADLEY is solicitous to explain that he rests his "old-fashioned notions" on the English

---

* S evens v. Adams. 23 Wend., 57; 26 Wend., 451; Balsfaugh v. Fraser, 19 Penn., 95; Webb v. Browning, 14 Mo., 355; In re Paschal, 10 Wall., 483, 494.

law of champerty, and he quotes from HOBART, BROOKE and BLACKSTONE to show that he states his legal propositions correctly. He cites DOMAT also, to prove that the same rule is recognized in the civil law. The simple answer to this pedantic display of foreign citations is, that neverthless such is *not* the law prevailing in this country. The courts in many States—and where the courts have hesitated the local legislatures—have generally concurred with the Federal tribunals in refusing to recognize the English statutes of champerty as a part of our law.* Are not "old-fashioned notions" based on obsolete laws quite as likely to be tainted with error as the prevailing views and customs of modern life?

But it may be conceded that the laws of a country, at the time of their adoption, are the most reliable exponents of its public policy and morality. The ancient statutes of champerty may be regarded as fair indications of the public opinion of the age in

---

* Sedgwick *v.* Stanton, 14 N. Y., 289; Schomp *v.* Schenck, 40 N. J. Law, 195; Matthewson *v.* Fitch, 22 Cal., 86; Wright *v.* Meek, 3 Greene (Iowa), 472; Lytle *v.* State, 17 Ark., 608; Bayard *v.* McLean, 3 Harr. (Del.), 139; Cassedy *v.* Jackson, 45 Miss., 397; Richardson *v.* Rowland, 40 Conn., 565; Sherley *v.* Riggs, 11 Humph. (Tenn.), 53; Cain *v.* Monroe, 23 Ga., 82; Bentick *v.* Franklin, 38 Tex., 458; Wylie v. Cox, 15 How. (U. S.), 415; Wright *v.* Tebbitts, 1 Otto, 252; Stanton *v.* Embrey, 3 Otto, 548; Roberts *v.* Cooper, 20 How. (U. S.), 467; McPherson *v.* Cox, 6 Otto, 404.

which they were deemed useful and necessary. The application, however, of this principle to our present situation will result in the subversion of the theory it is invoked to sustain. The laws now and here (notably in New York and New Jersey) permit, by express legislation or judicial sanction, the same practices which were then and there prohibited. Therefore, according to Judge BRADLEY, it is proper and professional to do in our time that which the laws authorize and approve, as it was formerly unseemly and immoral to attempt to do what the laws prohibited. Would Judge BRADLEY accept decisions of medieval courts as authoritative and final on the various subjects of witchcraft, religious tests, imprisonment for debt, and other outgrowths of earlier ages? But similar changes have taken place with the development of modern society in reference to the laws of maintenance and champerty. Even in England the ideas of the times in which these laws had their birth have long since ceased to exert any influence with the public, although they still retain a technical foothold in Westminster Hall.

But I may not presume to enlarge on a topic to which I can apply the language of the foremost juridical philosopher of modern times. "Whether in the barbarous age which gave birth to these bar-

barous precautions—whether, even under the zenith
of feudal anarchy, such fettering regulations could
have had reason on their side, is a question of
curiosity rather than use. My notion is, that there
never was a time—that there never could have been
or can be a time—when the pushing of suitors away
from court with one hand, while they are beckoned
into it with the other, would not be a policy equally
faithless, inconsistent and absurd. But what every-
body must acknowledge is, that to the times which
called forth these laws, and in which alone they
could have started up, the present are as opposite
as light to darkness. A mischief, in those times it
seems but too common, though a mischief not to be
cured by such laws, was, that a man would buy a
weak claim in hopes that power might convert it
into a strong one, and that the sword of a baron,
stalking into court with a rabble of retainers at his
heels, might strike terror into the eyes of a judge
upon the bench. At present what cares an English
judge for the swords of a hundred barons? Neither
fearing nor hoping, hating nor loving, the judge of
our days is ready with equal phlegm to administer,
upon all occasions, that system, whatever it be, of
justice or injustice, which the law has put into his
hands. A disposition so consonant to duty could
not have then been hoped for: one more consonant

is hardly to be wished. *Wealth has indeed the monopoly of justice against poverty ; and such monopoly it is the direct tendency and necessary effect of regulations like these to strengthen and confirm. The law created this monopoly : the law, whenever it pleases, may dissolve it.*" * Thanks to the spirit of modern reform, our law has dissolved it, and, as I purpose to prove, in the interests of justice and civilization.

I proceed, then, to examine the arguments adduced for the conclusion, so formally announced, that the custom of receiving contingent fees is demoralizing and degrading to the legal profession.

The first and principal reason is, that it encourages litigation and disturbs the peace of society. This, it will be noted, is the old reason assigned for the enactment of the statutes of champerty, which is so summarily set aside by Jeremy Bentham. It has been the stock reason of sticklers for "old-fashioned notions" on nearly all the subjects of legal reform during the last hundred years. The negotiability of commercial paper, the right to assign contracts and to transfer causes of action, the competency of parties and persons in interest as witnesses, the abolition of forms and fictions and

---

3 Bentham's Works, 19. Bowr. Ed.

the union of procedures in law and equity, and last, but not least, the repeal of statutes regulating fees between attorney and client, were all strenuously opposed, because they aoffrded additional facilities to the "pests of society," and tended to increase the "evil" of litigation. This, indeed, is the common ground of assault upon the moral right of lawyers to engage at all in the practice of their profession. The common law, for the same reason, refused to recognise them as a class, or their right to represent their clients in the courts. A special license was necessary from the king, in each case, to entitle one person to appear for another in a civil action. The great inconvenience of this practice finally prevailed over the common prejudice, and it became customary to grant general licenses to a few favored persons to exercise these peculiar privileges. And it is only in very recent times that counsel have been permitted to appear for the accused in criminal prosecutions.

But it does not follow that a new rule or an old custom is objectionable because it adds to the conveniences or increases the amount of litigation. On the contrary such a result may often be conducive and even necessary to the general welfare, and may be properly considered its highest title to public

utility and approval.   The enlightened spirit of
the present age requires that every facility should
be furnished for the "speedy, universal and impartial administration of justice."   The organic theory
of the law is, that "where there is a legal right.
there is also a legal remedy," and the great desider-
atum in civil government is to ascertain the most
effectual method of affording the means of reparation for every infraction of the rights of the hum-
blest, as well as the most influential citizen.   Courts
and judges "have no justification for their existence, except as they fulfill this mission."   The
chief distinction between civilization and barbarism
is, that the former provides a civil remedy for every
injury to person or property, while the latter leaves
the sufferer without redress, except as he may be
able to enforce his rights by violence or stratagem.
In Russia, Turkey and Mexico justice is stagnant
and the law a farce.   In England and the United
States litigation is luxuriant.   Wherever, then,
wrongs are inflicted on individuals or classes, or
their civil rights are invaded, it is the primary object of a wise and just public policy to afford them
prompt and efficient legal redress, and to encourage
them to seek such redress, rather than resort to barbarous methods, by making the courts easy of access, and leaving the suitors free to enter into such

arrangements as their circumstances may require to enable them to prosecute their claims with vigor and success.*

But the principal point of this objection as stated by Judge Cooley is, the injustice resulting to corporations from actions brought against them for negligence. This is the burden of complaint on the part of the officers and agents of these corporations, as well as by their representatives at the bar and on

---

* Chancellor Sandford, of New York, in delivering the opinion of the Court of Errors in Thallhimer *v.* Brinckerhoff, 3 Cow., 604, 653, gives the true reason of the old English rule: "Champerty, maintenance, and barratry were defined as offences in very early stages of English law. These practices seem to have been common in England; and they were denounced not only as sins very heinous in themselves, and highly injurious to the peace of society, but also as offences which actually interrupted the course of public justice." "*Feeble, partial and corrupt must have been the administration of justice, where such a reason could have force*" "The excitement of suits is an evil when suits are unjust; but when right is withheld, and the object of a suit is *just*, to promote the suit is to *promote justice.* That a resort to the public tribunals for justice should produce injustice, can be true, *only where the administration of justice is weak and corrupt,* or where the laws are very imperfect. Where the administration of justice is *firm, pure, and equal to all,* and where the laws give adequate redress for groundless suits, it is not easy to conceive, that mischief can arise from opening the courts of justice to all suitors, or from *contracts by which the fruits of a suit may be divided between him who has the right of action, and him who has contributed advice, expense or exertion, to institute the suit, or prosecute it to effect.*" Whatever may be the views of the members of this special commission on the subject, I think the great body of the profession have unfailing confidence in the ability, firmness and integrity of American courts of justice.

the bench. Judge COOLEY formulates these complaints with admirable complacency, when he
charges that these actions, as a rule, "are instituted in reliance, not upon justice or the law of
the case, but upon the effect of appeals to passion
or prejudice. These are often taken as mere ven-
tures—as one might invest in a lottery ticket, or in
the exploration of an unknown land for possible
mineral wealth. Perhaps no other class of suits
does so much toward bringing the jury system into
contempt, or toward creating a feeling of antagon-
ism between aggregated capital on the one side and
the community in general on the other.  *  *  *
In no small degree this affects the public confidence
in legal proceedings; corporations are made to believe that justice for them is not to be obtained from
juries, and the public is made to believe that courts
very often improperly interpose to annul just verdicts against great corporate monopolies."  No one
ought to know better than Judge COOLEY, to what
extent public confidence is affected or impaired in
the State of Michigan by the methods there pursued in administering justice between corporations
and individuals.  But if he intends to give his remarks a wider application, it is due to truth and
justice to state that his language is an unwarranted
imputation, equally on the courts of the country

and the " community in general."   I can, at least,
assure him that there is not the slightest ground for
suspicion, much less for such an imputation against
the courts of New York.   Nor is there any greater
reason to attribute to disappointed litigants or attorneys in this "class of suits," a disposition to
charge their misfortunes to the improper interfer-
ence of the courts.   Our judges, with rarely an exception, have shown a marked freedom from bias or
prejudice in the treatment of corporation cases.
During an experience at the bar extending over a
quarter of a century, I have never heard a whisper
of dissatisfaction, in this respect, with the decisions
of our tribunals.   The profession and the courts
get along together quite as well in this class of cases
as any other ; trials are conducted, exceptions taken
to rulings, appeals brought and heard, and decisions
rendered and received in the same spirit of kindness and courtesy on the one side and of deference
and respect on the other, which usually characterize
all other judicial proceedings.

But, if it were otherwise, the bench are not as
dependent on the bar as Judge COOLEY seems to imagine.   The judge is pre-eminently the architect of
his own fame and fortune.   He alone, of all his fellows in public or private life, is entrusted with the
power of protecting himself while preserving and

enforcing the rights of others. He is the ultimate and supreme oracle of the sovereign will, who has only to exercise his functions in the spirit of justice, freedom and independence, to secure the approval and applause of all impartial citizens. It is the judicial weathercock, who panders to the passing wave of popular passion or sentiment, and truckles to social, corporate or political influence, that is sure to incur, in the end, public censure and condemnation. Nor is it a good sign to see a judge, in the performance of his judicial duties, attempting to feel his way too assiduously with the profession. Let him act and decide with proper firmness and independence as well as impartiality, neither counting upon commendation nor caring for criticism, and he need not fear that the ebullitions of displeasure of a few disappointed spirits "will weaken his hold upon the public confidence," or on the "moral support" he will be sure to receive from the profession at large.

I will not, however, deny that Judge COOLEY states with substantial accuracy the mood of opposition and contempt for the jury system, manifested by the officers and attorneys of corporate monopolies.* The painful feature of this portion of his re-

---

* A comparison of the expressions above quoted from Judge COOLEY's "disinterested and authoritative opinion," as it is la-

marks, consists in the earnest and even enthusiastic tone of approval with which he greets these wanton misrepresentations. If he is justly indignant that interested lawyers should indorse their clients' passionate "censures" of the court, what is the proper measure of condemnation to be passed upon a judge, "who, unaffected by the interest or passion of parties, ought unhesitatingly to give the jury his moral support, is found himself" approving these "expressions of disappointment and anger"?—an approval, I am constrained to add, "which is vastly more effective in weakening the hold of the jury system upon public confidence, than could be any complaints of corporation suitors or attorneys whose interests are known to be at stake." If it be indecorous and unprofessional for a lawyer, in an outburst of passion, to privately impugn the motives of the court in rendering a decision, to what extent is a judge amenable to the same reproof, who deliberately pens in his private study, for publication in the press, an atrocious calumny on his co-laborers in the administration of justice?

Doubtless, juries in this, as in other classes of litigation — sometimes from misapprehension, and

---

belled in the Law Journal, with the fierce and frantic screed of ex-Judge HAND (see Appendix),—a very eminent corporation attorney—will, in this connection, be found interesting and suggestive.

even from passion and prejudice — have rendered
verdicts not warranted by evidence.  But have not
judges often done likewise?  Are not the law reports replete with illustrations of human frailty on
the bench?  The practiced eye of the advocate de-
tects the waywardness of incorrigible human nature
on the bench quite as frequently as in the jury box.

But let us examine more minutely this grave judicial imputation on the jury system in connection with corporation cases.  Judge COOLEY, in his
"opinion," has raised this issue as the pivotal point
in the discussion.  He builds his argument on this
foundation.  He instances this "class of suits" as
proof of the "corrupting" tendencies of contingent
fees.  He distinctly suggests, if he does not charge
in terms, that these particular cases are conceived
in iniquity, and are successfully carried by the con-
nivance of juries through the courts.  Ex-Judge
HAND voices the same accusation with special em-
phasis, as follows:  "It is *said* that worthless persons, having nothing, risking nothing, are induced
under this system to present and swear through
simulated causes of action, relying upon attorneys
to furnish all necessary moneys and divide the
profits if successful."  If this be true, it ought to
be susceptible of reasonable proof.  Nothing is
offered in the line of evidence, except what "is

said" by corporation attorneys and agents, who are paid as lawyers and lobbyists for saying and repeating it on all public and private occasions.* And now that this malevolent charge has been adopted and indorsed in an extra-judicial "opinion," it ought to be verified and established or frankly disavowed. I ask, then, for the proof. Has Judge COOLEY any personal or judicial knowledge of facts or circumstances on which to predicate this charge? Let him name the instances or cases within his own experience or reported in the books. He owes it to his own judicial character to support the charge by tangible evidence, or to retract it as publicly as he made it.

In the meantime, it may serve to throw some ad-

---

* Entertaining evidence of this fact is furnished by the columns of the Law Journal during the months of June and July, 1881. The numerous contributions on this subject from corporation attorneys, amply attest their fealty and fidelity to their employers. The only surprising feature is, that so many of them attempted concealment under anonymous signatures One bold and aspiring gentleman, however, offered a novel suggestion which is worthy of preservation. He would limit contingent fees to the "ablest" lawyers! That I may not do him injustice, I will quote his language: "There are cases where it is a necessity that the compensation of counsel should be contingent, for the reason that clients sometimes have rights to be protected or enforced, which require the services of the *ablest* counsel at our bar; and yet, they being poor, are entirely unable to command *such services*, except it be on an agreement for compensation contingent upon success, but *they* are the exception to the rule!" The *poor* attorneys, of course, must work for nothing.

ditional light on the subject and to hasten the final
result of the investigation, to introduce a counterclaim relating to the rights, interests and methods
of these "corporate monopolies." Cases of negligence against corporations arise, first and princi-
pally, with their agents and servants; secondly,
with persons to whom they owe special duties, as
passengers; and thirdly, with strangers. Their
legal relations and responsibilities to these various
classes of persons, are precisely the same as those
of one citizen or individual, under the same circumstances, to another. But it is obvious that their
general power and influence are far superior, as
well as their facilities for exerting control over
those with whom they come in close or casual con-
tact. Union is power in legal controversy not less
than in commercial rivalry or political strife—the
association of persons and the accumulation of
wealth, within the range of legitimate effort, enable
the corporate entity to employ talents and experience, to incur expenditures, and to resort to expedients, beyond the means of their opponents. They
have also ample opportunity in litigation, for the
illegitimate exertion of their ascendency and control, in manipulating their servants as witnesses
and in resorting to all the technical devices of professional strategy, to obtain delay and to necessitate

expense for their opponents. Their power over
their employés, for all practical purposes, is absolute; and these employés have the best opportunities for information, and where one of themselves
is the victim, are generally the only persons having
personal knowledge of the facts and circumstances
involved in the controversy. Their legal contests
are always conducted with unceasing vigilance and
vigor, never yielding short of the last resort, or
while an expedient remains untried, to exhaust the
patience or tax the resources of their adversaries.
Their agents are adepts in the art of intimidation,
and are profuse with threats of endless and expensive litigation to all who are reluctant to comply
with their demands, or to submit to their impositions; and it is a rule of corporate policy, to make
a legal contest ruinous to the rash contestant who
presumes to summon them into the courts. Is it
strange that even men of standing and substance,
with claims whose legality is incontestable, are loth
to engage in legal strife with such persistent and
powerful antagonists? Few men have the courage
and tenacity to press a valid claim in the courts,
with the moral certainty that it will be desperately
fought and its enforcement, after infinite annoyance
and delay, be more burdensome in a pecuniary
sense than its abandonment.

But what is the position of the poor employé or passenger, who is injured through corporate negligence, or of his family, in case the injury results in death? They have no means to carry on a litigation—much less to fee attorneys—no friends who can render them any available assistance, and no other resource than to interest, if possible, some courageous lawyer in their behalf. What is their remedy? Two suggestions are offered as to the proper course to pursue under these circumstances: 1. That the company could probably be induced to .compromise a fair and honest claim. 2. That the lawyer should accept the proffered employment as a case of charity, or rely on the gratitude of the client for his remuneration after a fortunate result. Both of these suggestions are founded on whimsical ideas of human nature, which might possibly be pardoned in inexperienced youths or visionary enthusiasts. They are simply absurd as emanations from men of any familiarity with public or private affairs. It is common experience in all the other departments of industry and enterprise, that men have difficulties and disagreements which can only be satisfactorily determined in the courts. Corporations and individuals often refuse to recognize their legal obligations without judicial compulsion. And clients, like other employers, frequently refuse to meet, not merely the claims of honor and gratitude, but other valid indebtedness, which can only be enforced in legal proceedings. There is no reason to suppose that claims and obligations growing out of the negligence of corporations, either as between the individual and the company or the claimant and his attorney, stand, in this respect, on any different footing.

Indeed, so far as the corporation and the individual are concerned, if such a case can be regarded as exceptional, the exception clearly points in the opposite direction ; for corporations, as a rule, are less inclined to regard with favor claims made against them on account of negligence than any other class of indebtedness. Besides (and this is the essence of the counterclaim), corporations frequently resort not only to the ordinary processes of litigious obstruction and delay, but to *active corruption and perjury* to defeat honest claims against them of this character. This serious charge ought not to be preferred on common rumor, or the hearsay of enraged and interested parties and their attorneys. It must, therefore, be supported by positive proof and record evidence of the highest authority or it shall be withdrawn. What is the proof?

In the official report of the case of *Ernst* v. *The Hudson River Railroad Company,*\* Judge PORTER,

---

\* 35 N. Y., 9. The action was brought by a widow to recover delivering the unanimous judgment of the court of dernier resort in the State of New York, uses this emphatic language: "It seems that the plaintiff was surprised on the former trial by proof, which she probably had no reason to expect, but which was not repeated on the last trial, when she was prepared with evidence to meet it. The prevailing opinion (on the former appeal) assumes—and we are at liberty, and perhaps bound, to suppose that the testimony of Simmons, Butler and Waltemyre, whom the defendent did not call on the last trial, justified the assumption—that Ernst was intoxicated on the occasion of the collision; that he drove so carelessly by the way that he nearly tipped over; that he was cautioned at the time by the person riding with him to drive more carefully; that he was partially deprived of the use of his ordinary faculties; that he knew the stated times for the passage of the trains; that this was, in fact, a regular train, on its stated and customary time; that it was notoriously due at that hour; that Dearstyne's hotel, at which Ernst stopped, was 150 feet east of the track; that he started from there at a rapid rate of speed; that other persons heard the train coming at quite a distance; that *four* of them, after he

damages for the negligent killing of her husband, as a traveller, at a railroad crossing.

started from the tavern, respectively called to him in a loud voice to stop, several times each ; that quite a number of persons saw the approach of the train ; and that he had an open view of it, nearly all the way from the hotel to the crossing, for a distance of a hundred rods from the highway on which he was riding. In the light of the evidence given on the last trial, it is not difficult to infer why testimony like this was not reproduced, when the plaintiff was prepared to meet it. * * *

Such testimony, though not met by a point blank contradiction, (on the former trial,) was too improbable in its nature, and too inconsistent with the other facts proved, either to obtain credence with the jury, or to commend itself to the full confidence of practiced jurists. * * * It now appears that the prominent facts then relied on to inculpate the testator were *fictitious*. Instead of being a drunkard, stupefied or crazed with liquor, he is proved to have been an orderly, sober and respectable citizen. The pretense that he drank anywhere that morning is abandoned, and his family physician testifies that he never knew him to be intoxicated. Instead of being deprived of the use of his faculties, he is shown to have been a man in the prime of life, of regular habits, with clear vision, and in perfect health. Instead of running his horses by the way, and starting from the tavern with reckless speed, he is shown to have been an experienced and practiced driver; and it is proved that, on this occasion, he started from the hotel on a walk, and continued to drive with moderation, prudence and judgment. The claim that he knew the stated times of the trains is also abandoned. The fact that this was a regular train, on its customary time, is alleged by none, even of the defendant's witnesses, except Gregory the engineer; and he is contradicted by Dearstyne, an intelligent and disinterested witness, who knew the time of the trains, etc. * * * It now appears that, instead of the testator's riding 150 feet in full view of the engine, the whole distance from the hotel to the track is less than 113 feet, and that he did not see the train at all, until it emerged from behind the station house, when the horses were in the very act of going upon the crossing. It also appears that, instead of his having, from the hotel down, except opposite the station house, an open view of the northern track for 100 rods, there was but one place in the whole distance where, even if he had been standing up and expecting a train, he could have seen it as far north as the ice-house, which was within 594 feet of the crossing. The track, instead of being straight, was sharply curved. The view, instead of being open, was obstructed by intervening woods and upland. * * * There is no pretense now that any one east of the store which adjoins the track, either saw or heard the train at all until it reached the crossing. * * * The claim that four men were hallooing to Ernst to stop, when he was not yet half way down, is also now abandoned. * * * The proof is clear and decisive, that the bell was not rung nor the whistle blown until after the collision. Only two of the defendant's witnesses claimed that they were; and they were the two employés whose neglect of that duty cost Ernst his life. * * * Both were impeached on material points, by their own oaths before the coroner's jury. * * * On the last trial it also appeared that this was a flag station; that it was the known and uniform practice of the company, whenever there was a train advancing within 80 rods of.the crossing on either side, to give notice to the public of its approach by exhibiting, at that point, a white flag if the engine was to stop, and a red flag if it was to pass without stopping. There was neither flag nor flagman at the crossing; and thus the practice, which was adopted for the security of the traveller, was converted on this occasion into a snare for his destruction."*

---

* 35 N. Y., 21–25.

In the light of this judicial conviction of a delib-
arate attempt on the part of this corporation to
"swear through a simulated defence, relying upon
attorneys to furnish all necessary" legal legerde-
main, and upon its employés to supply the "fictitious" facts, let us look a little farther into the
history of this case for evidence of corporate methods and management. The accident occurred in
December, 1855, and the action was commenced in
1856. On the first trial at the Circuit, in May,
1859, the plaintiff was nonsuited. The Supreme
Court, on appeal, set aside the nonsuit.* The
second trial in February, 1861, resulted in a verdict
of $2,500 for the plaintiff. The judgment entered
on the verdict was affirmed by the Supreme Court,
but reversed by the Court of Appeals and a new
trial ordered.† The third trial in November, 1865,
resulted in a second judgment of nonsuit, which
was affirmed in the Supreme Court. But the judgment was again reversed by the Court of Appeals.‡
On the fourth trial the plaintiff recovered a judgment of $5,000, which was sustained in the Supreme
Court, and in March, 1868, finally affirmed by the
Court of Appeals.§ Thus, after a fiercely fought
contest of twelve years duration, the widow main-

---

* 32 Barb., 159.        † 24 How. Pr. R., 97.
‡ 35 N. Y., 10.        § 39 N. Y., 61.

tained her claim against the company. But even after the solemn judgment of the highest appellate court, convicting the company of subornation of perjury, it did not yield an iota, but stubbornly persisted in a hopeless struggle through another trial and another series of appeals to the same tribunal of last resort!

The case of *Gale* v. *The New York Central and Hudson River Railroad Company*,* affords corroborative proof of the same high character. It also proves that the successor of the old company, though it has passed under a new regime, still recognizes the common code of corporate ethics, and pursues the old iniquitous course of dealing with this class of cases. The accident occurred in July, 1873. The plaintiff, a reputable farmer of very little means, after several months confinement to his room—although his injuries lamed him for life, and incapacitated him to pursue his calling—was so reluctant to commence an action that his counsel, on his behalf, offered to accept the paltry sum of $600 in satisfaction of his claim; a sum barely sufficient to pay his medical and other expenses, and loss of time during his illness. This

---

* 76 N. Y., 594. The action was brought by a traveller on the highway, to recover damages for a personal injury at a railroad crossing, caused by a defect in the roadway.

proposal was rejected, and finally in January, 1875, he resorted to legal proceedings. The trial took place in February, 1877, lasting twelve days, and resulted in a verdict of $14,000 for the plaintiff. The defendant moved before ·Mr. Justice WEST-BROOK, who presided on the trial, to set aside the verdict. The company not only raised all possible legal exceptions, but boldly imputed partiality and misconduct to the jury, introducing affidavits to sustain the charge, and also produced the deposition of ˙one White that he witnessed the accident, and saw the plaintiff drive to one side instead of directly over the crossing, so that his wagon wheels struck the rails south of the planking, thus causing the accident by his own negligence ; and he further deposed that to avoid being a witness he had not informed the defendant of these facts until after the trial. The company, therefore, based its application particularly on the grounds of misconduct on the part of the jury and of newly discovered evidence. The plaintiff produced the depositions of two persons, that at the time of the accident White was at work with them in an adjoining town, seven miles distant from the crossing ; of five persons that he was a "vagabond" whose word or oath was utterly worthless ; of four persons, that he had been guilty of petit larceny on three different occa-

sions ; and of two persons, that he had been charged
under oath by his own daughter with attempting to
violate her person, and "ran away to avoid arrest."*
The motion was promptly denied by the circuit
judge, who repelled the imputation on the jury, as
follows: "It is proper to state that the jury was
selected with great care, each one being carefully
examined. Their answers and appearance showed
them to be men of more than average character and
intelligence. Nothing occurred upon the trial to
cause the court to suspect their impartiality."†
Mr. Justice LEARNED, speaking for the Supreme
Court on appeal, in affirming the decision of the
circuit judge, thus refers to the newly discovered
evidence: "The testimony and the character of the
witness (White) are attacked so severely as to show
that little confidence can be placed in the new evidence which the defendant desires to introduce."‡
And this judgment was in January, 1879, affirmed
by the Court of Appeals.§

Does it become a corporation attorney to charge
the wrongs and offences of his own client upon the
luckless victims of corporate carelessness and cru-

---

* These affidavits are contained in the Error Book on appeal.
See vol. 622, Court of Appeals Cases in the State Library.

† 53 How. Pr. R , 395.

‡ 13 Hun, 7.

§ 76 N. Y , 594.

elty? Does it denote a spirit of judicial candor, to adopt "these sayings" of interested litigants and zealous attorneys without verification or proof? I do not mean to intimate that this particular company is either better or worse than the average corporation. I cite the cases in which it was concerned, because its attorneys have been conspicuous in charging perjury and fraud upon those whom it has refused to recompense for injuries received through its negligence. Other similar cases might be mentioned, but my purpose is accomplished in showing that the countercharge is not, like the original ones of Judges COOLEY and HAND, a random assertion, unsupported by proof.

Nor is this method of treating this class of claims surprising, when the policy pursued by corporations in selecting legal representatives, is considered. Let us take, again, as an illustration, the client of ex-Judge HAND, one of the most powerful "corporate monopolies" in the country. It employs at the head of its law department a reputable gentleman at a large salary, who really has no connection with its controversies in the courts. It retains for this purpose a large number of local attorneys, living along the line of the road from New York to Buffalo. The chief of the department distributes the cases to these attorneys, being governed largely in the selection by the venue of the action or the place of the accident. In the city of Albany it retains three leading law firms, whose members respectively belong to the opposing political parties. These local attornies, who represent the company in all legal proceedings, receive no stated salaries, but special remuneration for services rendered. They are all, therefore, directly interested in contesting every claim presented against the company. If there is no contest, there is no compensation to be earned. All corporation attorneys are conscientiously opposed to contingent fees. They are liberally rewarded in any event; and it is of no concern to them whether the result is favorable or not. It follows, that nearly every claim is likely to be reported by the vigilant attorney as a monstrous case of "simulation"—a corrupt "speculation" between the claimant and his attorney to "swindle" the company; and the defendant is advised that the suit must be defended at all hazards, by way of "example," etc. The result may be easily conjectured. The case is contested inch by inch through all the courts. The plaintiff finally recovers at least twice as much as he would gladly have accepted in compromise at the outset. And then the company pays the amount of the claim the third time to its attor-

ney, as an expression of its gratitude for his zealous
and efficient services. In the Ernst case, it is safe
to assume that the company paid in expenses and
costs twice or three times as much as the plaintiff
finally recovered. And in the Gale case, which it
might have settled at the outset for $600, it was
compelled to pay about $17,000 in the end, besides
its own costs and expenses, which may be estimated
at several thousand more. The legal expenses of
the company are enormous, under such a system,
and the damages and costs collected by legal process are doubtless treble the amount at which they
could be compromised, if the company were governed by a wise policy of prompt recognition and
payment of honest claims *

These observations develope very clearly that the
general policy of corporations, is to litigate this

---

* The charge of "speculation," in the case of a contingent fee,
comes from corporation attornies with exceeding bad grace. It
may be safely affirmed that, in a great majority of instances, the
position of attorney to such an institution is procured through the
most laborious effort or manipulation of persons and interests;
and the attorney, or some relative, is usually a stockholder and
often a director or trustee, for the mere purpose of securing or
controlling the position. Instead of following the practice of his
profession and receiving retainers from the corporation in the
usual manner, he is too often a rapacious legal "operator" or
"wrecker," who speculates in its stock merely to obtain, under
the name of fees or costs, his share of irregular dividends.

class of claims without reference to their merits.* The instances are very rare where compromises are effected, and many companies do not hesitate to avow, as a settled rule of policy, their purpose to contest all claims of this character. If, therefore, corporations can succeed in preventing lawyers from making such reasonable arrangements with injured persons to render them professional assistance, as their circumstances will warrant, substantial immunity will be secured from all legal liability for corporate negligence. If the injured party is compelled to pay or secure a definite fee to his lawyer in advance, in nine cases in ten, he will be unable to prosecute his claim. Corporations will in this way obtain complete exemption from responsibility for negligence to their employés, as well as to a very large proportion of the traveling and general public.

---

* If Judge COOLEY has any doubt on this point, he would do well to consult the editor of the Law Journal, who has had large experience in the prosecution of these cases. While he was at the bar and "in the habit of making a great deal of money out of this mode of practice," he published to the world, that "the very wealth which would enable the negligent party to respond in damages would deter the injured party from entering upon a long and expensive litigation. It is notorious that no judgment can be collected of a railroad company, except at the very end of the law's rope." Brown's Humorous Phases of the Law, 90, 91. Candor, however, requires me to add his subsequent confession, that he was then unable to "see this matter in its real *moral* bearings." 24 Albany Law Journal, 5.

Aside from the frightful amount of injustice which would thus be perpetrated and permitted without redress, the inevitable result of pursuing such a policy for any considerable period, would be fraught with serious dangers to the social organism. The only efficacious punishment that can now be imposed upon these corporations, is to coerce pecuniary recompense to the sufferers. Where this remedy is most rigidly enforced, the natural tendency is still so strong to apathy and indifference to the rights of others, in the absence of a sense of personal responsibility, that it is with the greatest difficulty corporations can be kept within any tolerable limits of restraint. It is a propensity of human nature to exercise power without reference to right, and it rarely fails to pass to the verge of endurance on the one hand and impunity on the other. An officer or agent of a corporation desiring to accomplish a particular purpose, or to gratify his vanity and convenience, by sending a special train of cars over its road at the highest rate of speed, simply ignoring its own rules and the safety of innocent persons, rarely hesitates to exercise the power regardless of the consequences. The casual convenience of a board of directors on a pleasure excursion, is often deemed an adequate reason for risking the limbs and lives of all those persons who, in the pursuit of their usual avocations, and acting on the assumption that the corporation will recognize its legal obligations, are unexpectedly brought into con-tact with its resistless agencies. By removing, then, the only remaining check upon corporatate negli-gence, human life would be subjected to still greater and more reckless sacrifices than it now is. The patience of the populace would soon become ex-hausted, if legal reparation were unattainable, and, fomenting into fury, would burst all the barriers of law and order. Coporate carelessness and in-difference to the rights of the public, would term-inate in popular tumults and riotous efforts at re-taliation and reprisal.

The other alternative, that lawyers are morally bound to recognize this portion (including the great majority) of the community as proper subjects of professional charity, who are entitled to demand their services *ad libitum* in the prosecution of these claims, is equally impracticable and absurd. The idea is founded on a totally false conception of the relation of attorney and client in modern society. Whatever may have been the nature of this rela-tion in the past, or whatever it may be now in other countries where the community is divided into guilds and classes, it certainly implies with us nothing of a political, public or social character. There is no legal or social bond of connection between the parties involving the general duty of defence on one side or dependence on the other. Their only public tie is that of a common citizenship, equal as well in immunities and rights as in duties and obligations. It is simply a private relation, the result of mutual consent, for reciprocal behoof and benefit. There is no moral duty or constraint, on either side, to enter into this relation in any particular case. A layman is under no obligation to retain a particular lawyer, or, for that matter, to retain any lawyer, in his litigations. He may appear in his own behalf in the courts as he may exercise in person any other legal right. Nor is a lawyer under any greater obligation to accept a particular retainer. He may reject offered employment for any reason satisfactory to himself, relating to the client or the case.

The principal exception to this rule is only applicable to this as to every other relation in life. Every member of society ought to be kind and generous to the poor and charitable in his dealings with the destitute A lawyer, therefore, should not refuse his services to one in indigent circumstances. Indeed, he is morally bound to render to one in need any reasonable assistance he may require. But no person is, in this sense, a proper subject of charity, who is able to earn a livelihood, or is interested in a valid claim against a responsible party, amounting to hundreds or thousands of dollars. The professional knowledge and ability of a lawyer, are his capital in business. In the greater number of cases he is in no better pecuniary circumstances than his client; and his labor is his only means of supporting himself and his family.* Is he under any moral coercion to donate his services to one who is as able to reward him as he is to labor without reward? If the client were the owner of a little property in possession or of an investment in public funds, it is generally conceded that it would be proper to secure a definite sum by contract for the services of the attorney. Where is the moral distinction between such a case and a contract securing compensation out of the claim in controversy? True, in the latter case it is contingent on success;† but as that is the best the client in his circumstances is able to offer, the.

---

\* There is no reason for supposing that lawyers are excepted from the anathema of St. Paul against those who provide not for their own households.

‡ The contingency would be the same whether there was an express contract, or it was left to legal implication, as the client in either event could not pay unless he was successful. The express agreement is only another mode of *securing* the attorney for his services, instead of paying him in advance. Christie *v.* Lawyer, 44 N. H., 298.

4

lawyer would not be justified in refusing to assist him. All the lawyer has a right to ask is an arrangement within the power of the client to make and perform. If he should press the client further, he would clearly be amenable to the charge of injustice and oppression. But the lawyer is under no higher obligation than any other member of the community, to labor without reward for those who are able directly or indirectly to secure him proper remuneration.

Moreover, this charitable idea is founded on a fanciful and fictitious view of human nature, whether we confine ourselves within or look beyond the bounds of our profession. Lawyers as a class are neither better nor worse than other groups of men in the same community. They have similar motives and aspirations in life, and need the same incentives to active duty. A practical rule of morals should be coincident with a sound public policy. We have seen that it is a favorite object of the civil power to afford the means of reparation, if sought within a reasonable period, for every legal injury. The theory of the law in real life, as in the moral world, although the recognition of offences is necessarily more limited, is that every wrong should be redressed unless it is voluntarily condoned. To give effect to this principle, it is essential to authorize and encourage a union of interests between those who suffer injuries and those who have the requisite skill—and may thus be induced—to aid in obtaining legal reparation. All past experience proves, as a rule, that persons unaffected by the wrongs or injuries of others will not deem it their duty to assume the burden of redressing them, unless it is made their interest to do so. To ignore this fact is sentimental folly or hypocritical cant.

If any proof is required of the truth of this view, it is to be found in the course pursued in reference to this class of claims, by those lawyers who pride themselves on their adherence to the old traditions. Why are these enthusiasts in the cause of charity content with "profane and vain bablings" concerning contingent fees when they have the simple remedy in their own hands? They have only to put their professions to the test. Let them personally engage in the prosecution of these corporation cases on the "no pay" plan, pure and simple. Human nature never fails to adjust itself to favorable circumstances, and is not reluctant to effect its purposes by the most available means within it reach. The owners of these claims will appreciate the boon, and will not hesitate to require their services. The "contingent business" will be irretrievably stamped out. And our professional monitors will

have laid up for themselves inestimable treasures
in the future.

The second reason urged against the propriety of
contingent fees, according to Judge COOLEY, is
"that they are corrupting, and affect injuriously
all the relations of the attorney." With Judge
BRADLEY, this is only another mode of stating
his principal ground of objection. He is opposed to the practice because it "promotes litigation," and "therefore is derogatory to the honor
of the profession." But this alleged tendency to
personal "corruption" is the central thought in
Judge COOLEY's share of the discussion. His
"opinion" is devoted to the task of elaborating
and enforcing this idea. To avoid inaccuracy, it
may be well to state his position in his own language. "A member of the bar is a minister of justice. He is licensed to assist the court in the administration of the law.   *   *   *   In the performance of his professional functions, the lawyer
owes duties to his client, to the court, and to the
State.   *   *   *   The lawyer's legitimate fee is
payable irrespective of the result, and he is supposed to occupy a position from which he can con-
template the controversy with a desire that the
correct rule of law shall be applied, and the truth

be expressed in the judgment, whether the result to his client be favorable or unfavorable. The policy of the law is, that neither his feelings nor his interest shall be so far enlisted as to tempt him to desire injustice ; but a contingent fee makes him·a party in desire and anxiety ; he becomes disqualified to be the adviser of the court, and the high sense of honor that should actuate all his professional conduct is blunted by the bribe that tempts his fidelity to justice.''

Who would imagine that this was the language of an experienced judge ? Who would not exclaim on hearing or reading the passage, without a knowledge of the author, that it was the effusion of a dreaming doctrinaire ? Clearly Judge COOLEY must have had a very limited experience at the bar, and as a nisi-prius judge. And a man may sit many years in an appellate court, listening to technical legal arguments and writing judicial opinions, without acquiring a practical knowledge of the duties and responsibilities of the profession. Judge COOLEY would raise members of the bar from the position of private citizens to the rank of public functionaries. He seems to regard their duties to their clients as merely incidental and subordinate to their more important public relations to the court and to the State. And he is deeply concerned that they should "enlist their selfishness" by accepting contingent fees for their services as "ministers of justice," so that "the court loses its proper reliance, and the State loses, in great measure, the advantages anticipated from this body of officers."

This is a most extraordinary misapprehension of the position and function of the lawyer in our society. He is not, in fact, a public officer or servant in any sense whatever. He is not selected, directly or indirectly, by any authoritative expression of the popular will—the source of all power and preferment. He holds no commission from any civil sovereignty. He is called to the performance of no public duty. He is entitled to his professional license as a personal right, which he can enforce by legal process, if he has complied with the conditions prescribed for all citizens. He cannot subsequently be deprived of this license, except for legal cause, after a trial and conviction. His diploma is required at the outset, merely to ascertain that he possesses the requisite qualifications to follow his vocation with credit to himself and benefit to his employers. He owes no different duties to the State than every other citizen.*

---

* Ex parte Garland, 4 Wall., 333; Matter of Cooper, 22 N. Y., 67; Blood, etc , County Judge Case, 33 Grat. (Va.), 443; Adm's of Byrne v Adm's of Stewart, 3 Desau. (S. C.), 466, 478; Leigh's Case, 1 Munf. (Va.), 468; Ingersoll v. Howard, 1 Heisk. (Tenn.),

Nor are his relations to the court of so menial a character as Judge COOLEY would have us believe. While the lawyer should always be frank, truthful and deferential, his highest duty will often require him to differ from the court, and to combat its tendencies with all the energies and resources at his command. He is the representative of his client, to present and protect *his* interests and to enforce what he believes to be his rights. If the judge is disposed to disagree with him, he is not to yield timorously and give the court his "generous support," but is bound to press his own views with firmness and fidelity to the end. He is not merely "to attend to the execution of the judgment which is awarded," but if he believes it to be erroneous, he ought to appeal from it and endeavor to correct the error. He is not and cannot be, in the performance of his professional duty, the "adviser" of the court. He is properly and necessarily identified in feeling and interest with his client's side of the case. He is, perhaps, aware of facts which, on account of some technical rule or unfortunate concurrence of circumstances, cannot be elicited in evidence, but are perfectly convincing to his own mind

247; Ex parte Faulkner, 1 West Va , 269; Ex parte Low, 35 Ga., 285; Ex parte Yale, 24 Cal., 242; Matter of Attorneys oaths, 20 Johns. (N. Y.), 491.

of the justness of his client's cause; and which
coerce him to struggle with the court to strain the
application of a legal principle in what he conceives
to be the interests of justice.   His special duty is to
secure, if possible, the rights of his client in the
particular case, while the court must also have an
eye to the general interests of justice and the effect
of the decision as a precedent in other cases.   The
lawyer believes in his client's integrity and good
faith.   He is biased by sympathy in favor of his
client's views, and, possibly, is also imbued with
his client's prejudices.   However honest and capable he may be, he is clearly under such circumstances the last person to act as the trusted "adviser" of the court.*

The veritable judge is bound to regard him as an
interested substitute or agent of the party, offering
in his name such suggestions as it may be supposed
the party would urge if acting in his own behalf.

---

* On this principle the courts will not trust or permit the attorney in a cause, nor even his partner, to act in any other capacity,
such as special master to execute the decree. or as receiver or attorney for the receiver.   White v. Haffaker, 27 Ill., 349; Bronck *v.*
Harrington, 49 How. (N. Y.), 196; Wilkinson *v.* Vorce, 41 Barb.
(N. Y.), 370; Spinks *v.* Davis, 32 Miss., 152.   " We cannot shut
our eyes to the fact that the law-partner of the solicitor is pre-
sumptively as much interested in the proceedings as the solicitor
himself, and it would be peculiarly objectionable that *he* should
act in a position requiring *impartiality.*"   COOLEY, J., in the case of
Merchants', etc., Bank of Detroit v. Kent, Judge, 43 Mich., 292, 297.

The judge must, therefore, listen not to the man or the lawyer, but to his arguments, as if they emanated directly from the party in interest. He must weigh in his own judicial balance not the advocate, but his reasons for or against a given proposition; and he must determine the controversy absolutely without reference to the position or power of the advocate. A competent judge will rely on the lawyer simply for information, not for "support;" and in utilizing the information he will endeavor to be blind to the source from which he received it. A judge abdicates his functions who allows an advocate to "hold his ear" or to lend him his "generous support." There are always "generous" men at the bar who are quite willing to be regarded as the "supporters" of the court, and I grieve to add that there is now and then a judge who is weak enough to lean on these "supports" for guidance through the mazes of legal controversy. But it is hardly necessary to remark that such a judge never rises very high in the judicial firmament.

The false premise thus inconsiderately assumed by Judge COOLEY, necessarily led to his untenable and absurd conclusion. Having metamorphosed the attorney into an assistant or advisory judge, his inference was unavoidable, that a fee from one of the parties, contingent on success, "disqualifies him to be the *adviser* of the court." I cheerfully concede that such an interest—or any interest in the way of compensation—renders the attorney unfit to sit in judgment on the merits of the case. And whenever the lawyer assumes to exercise such a prerogative, or the judge attempts to "advise" with and lean upon him for "support" in rendering the decision, it will be full time to interpose some effective barrier to preserve intact the administration of justice.

But let us come to close quarters with the main thesis of Judge COOLEY in this branch of the discussion. His position is, that "the lawyer's legitimate fee is payable irrespective of the result;" and the purport of his contention is, that any contingent *interest* in the litigation is "injurious" and "corrupting" to the profession. True to the last, in his efforts to "magnify his office," the learned judge insists that such an interest on the part of the lawyer "incapacitates him from performing the highest and most honorable of his duties, namely, those which are owing to the court and to the law itself."

I pause to award Judge COOLEY, among his colleagues in the commission, the palm of consistency. He has, at least, attempted to argue the question on principle, and he has conscientiously followed his methods of rationation to their legitimate results.

If his conclusions cannot be maintained, it is not from any syllogistic flaw in his deductions, but because his premises are preposterous. He improperly premises: 1. That the lawyer's highest duties are not to the client and himself, but to the court and the State; and, 2d, That the lawyer ought not to be identified in feeling or interest with his client's cause. Having disposed of the first, I now proceed to consider his second assumption.

What is the duty of the lawyer to his client? Happily this question is too well settled by the courts, in accordance with the obvious dictates of morality, to require more than a simple statement of the results of the adjudications. We have seen that it is optional with the lawyer whether he will consent to be retained in a particular case. If his judgment is convinced from the preliminary consultation that the cause is without any merit, he ought so to inform the party and to refuse the proffered employment. But if he accepts the retainer, the law attaches certain obligations which he cannot avoid. He undertakes that he is qualified to guard, and that he will exert his skill and exercise ordinary vigilance to protect his client's rights. He agrees that he will represent his client in the case, act for him in every stage of the litigation, and do in his behalf whatever he might lawfully do himself, and would be likely to do, if he were a reputable man familiar with legal proceedings and on the alert in his own interest. He gives to the client his sacred pledge of absolute fidelity to the trust reposed in him. If from ignorance of the law, or negligence in the conduct of the cause, or culpable "generosity" to the adversary or the judge, the rights of the client are sacrificed, the law holds the attorney responsible for the injury.* And the client promises on his part, in consideration of the faithful performance of the engagement, to reasonably remunerate the attorney for his services. Is it possible for a lawyer to contract such a relation in good faith, without feeling that his interests in the case are identified with those of his client? Aside from his sense of legal responsibility, his pride of professional success and the incitement of pecuniary recompense,—he has been taken into his client's confidence, impressed with his misfortune, aroused by his indignation or fired by his zeal; and he is not insensible to the compliment implied in his selection to the coveted post of professional duty. By accepting the retainer, the lawyer signifies to the

---

* Bonman v. Tallman, 2 Robts (N. Y.), 385; 3 Abb. Ct. of Ap., Dec. (N. Y.), 182, note; Ex'parte Giberson, 4 Cranch C. C. R., 503; Hatch v. Fogerty, 1 Jones & Spen. (N. Y. Superior Court), 166; Walpole v. Carlisle, 32 Ind., 415; Watson v. Muirhead, 57 Penn., 161.

court and to the world his confidence in the justness of his client's claim, and that he has undertaken to maintain it at the bar against all opposition.* If he is honest in his convictions and
faithful to his trust, he soon becomes as warmly
enlisted in behalf of his client as he could possibly
be if the case were his own. Indeed, it may be
safely asserted as an ascertained result of professional experience that a lawyer will fail to do his
full duty in a cause, unless he becomes thoroughly
imbued with his clients views and identified with
his interests.†

But this strenuous objection of Judge COOLEY, if
of any force, would extend much farther than he
attempts to apply it in his "opinion." It is equally
repugnant to the practice which is specially en-
dorsed as proper and professional by his associates.
The tendency to "corruption" and the temptation

---

* I refer only to civil actions. There may be some exceptions
to this rule, but they are very rare as between the plaintiff and his
attorney. It is, however, proper and often necessary to interpose
a defence to a valid claim because it is exorbitant etc., or is made
the basis of improper relief.

† Lest this remark should lead to misapprehension. it is proper
to note that I am merely stating the rule without the exceptions or
qualifications. I am assuming that nothing occurs in the progress
of the cause to arouse the suspicion or weaken the confidence of
the attorney in the integrity of his client. When, however, this
occurs, the lawyer must adapt his line of conduct to the change of
circumstances.

to pervert legal processes to purposes of injustice, are just as strong where the attorney performs the service with the expectation of varying his charge with the degree of success as where he agrees to do so at the outset. In either event the amount of his fee—and if the client has no other means than the claim or property in suit, his entire fee—depends on the result of the litigation ; and, according to Judge COOLEY, "the high sense of honor that should actuate his professional conduct is blunted by the bribe that tempts his fidelity to justice." Ex-Judge DILLON states it as a fact (and every lawyer of any experience will confirm his statement), that it is a prevailing custom at the bar "to charge more for the same skill and labor where they lead to a successful result than where they do not." This practice is not limited to poor clients, but includes "most professional charges." The profession at large, then, do not deem it dishonorable (having possibly "become untrustworthy in judgment from permitting their sense of honor and fidelity to be subordinated to their personal interests"), to "enlist their selfishness" in their clients' causes by making their charges "proportioned to the degree of success ;" and if there is any real foundation for the imputations of Judge COOLEY, they are, as a body (ex-Judge DILLON being the witness), a'most disreputable class of men—corrupt gamblers and traders, who cheat their clients, deceive the courts, and keep society in perpetual strife for their own selfish purposes. Indeed, this unassuming triune man,— judge, lecturer and author (as we are informed by the Law Journal), in order to vindicate "legal verities," deals out defamation to all who have occasion to assist the courts in administering justice with as much composure as he would set aside a verdict in a case of negligence against a corporation, or condemn a prize in a lottery. He has an undisguised contempt for the "jury system;" and he denounces without stint all lawyers who accept fees measured by or dependent on the result * as bribe-takers, who antagonize the interests of their clients, manipulate juries, slander judges, and bring the courts into public disrepute! One is tempted to ask, "upon what meat doth this our Ceasar feed that he is grown so wise?"

But it is necessary to advance still another step to expose, in all its nakedness, the personal position of this distinguished judge. While as a professor or doctrinaire, he dooms all that portion of the profession to outer darkness who do not limit themselves to "fees payable irrespective of the result,"

---

* Ex-Judge DILLON says most of them do it.

incredible as it may seem, he holds in his judicial capacity that their "legitimate fees" *are* properly affected and determined by the degree of success! Judge COOLEY himself assisted in establishing the doctrine, now prevailing throughout the country, that the final *result* of a litigation is one of the proper *elements* to be recognized in ascertaining the value of legal services. In an action to recover for such services, in the absence of a special agreement, the Supreme Court of Michigan, MARSTON, J., delivering the opinion,* approved the following rule: "In all cases the professional skill and standing of the person employed, his experience, the nature of the controversy, both in regard to the amount involved and the character and nature of the questions raised, *as well as the result*, must all be taken into consideration in fixing the value of the services rendered." Judge COOLEY as one of the members of the court concurred in this decision. He holds, then, as a judge, that a lawyer may render his ser-

---

* Eggleston *v.* Baldwin, 37 Mich., 14, 18. In the language of FOSTER J. in Phelps *v.* Hunt, 40 Conn., 97, 101: "In law as in war success is one test of ability. The military man who wins many victories will be called an able general, and a lawyer who is pressed with professional engagements shows one of the incidents of legal eminence." And it was accordingly held that the amount of his business etc., was a proper element in ascertaining the value of his services.

vices on the assumption that he will be paid
more if he succeeds than if he fails, and that it is
right, even against the protests of the client, to consider the final result in determining the amount of
his compensation. But as a theorist, he declares
that if an attorney, at the request of his client, in
accordance with this legal principle, agrees to accept
the same rate of remuneration, "he permits his
sense of honor and professional fidelity to be subordinated to his personal interests," and loses all
claim to consideration and respect from his brethren of the bar! The lawyer, according to this
theory, has no moral right to stipulate with his client beforehand for the identical fee which he has a
perfect right to claim and enforce in the end against
the persistent objections of his employer! Does
Judge Cooley imagine that the demoralizing influence or the selfish incentive to undue professional
exertion, will be affected by the fact that his contingent interest is expressly recognized by contract
or is left to be enforced by legal process? Does not
Judge Cooley's rule of law for ascertaining the
value of legal services, according to his own principles, necessarily tend to encourage professional immorality? And if a lawyer, who accepts his clients
proposal for a fee gauged by the result, is justly
amenable to all of Judge Cooley's denunciations,

5

does not a judge, who entertains such an opinion and yet judicially approves the vicious principle and enforces it against a resisting client, really merit impeachment?

Is there any more reason for Judge COOLEY's assault upon lawyers who accept contingent fees, in reference to their private dealings with their clients? The following is another characteristic specimen of his style of vituperation: "Such a practice tempts lawyers to deal deceitfully with those who go to them for advice, to express doubts of results when they feel none, to suggest difficulties which they do not really anticipate, to] magnify the probable cost of litigation; in short to do anything rather than express a frank opinion of the actual case and its probabilities, with a view if possible to bring the client to the point of proposing a part of the property or damages claimed, if by means thereof he shall be put in possession of the remainder. If, for example, the lawyer can so far discourage his client as to obtain from him an offer of one half of property worth $20,000, for the performance of services worth not to exceed $500, and success seems reasonably certain, he is manifestly interested to the extent of $9,500, to deal disengenuously with his client. \* \* \* If suit is instituted without any such arrangement, there is then the temptation to permit delays, annoyances, trouble and cost to the client that might be avoided, with a view to the same end; and no doubt some lawyers who consider themselves highminded and honorable unconsciously lose the spur to diligence in their suits when discouragement to their clients seems likely to prove more profitable to them than would the energetic pursuit of a remedy.''

If Judge Cooley, in this extract, is relating his own personal experience at the bar, he is, of course, entitled to the same credit as any other convert or pervert who ''meets with a change'' in later years, and deems it desirable to impress his new set or coterie by the recital of stirring reminiscences of ''trespasses and sins'' in his earlier career. But, giving full faith to his narrative, even in that view, instead of proving a prevailing practice on the part of a particular class of lawyers to swindle their clients, it merely uncovers an isolated case of individual demoralization. Doubtless such cases occasionally occur in all trades and professions, and among those who receive contingent fees at the bar\* as well

---

* As I wish to deal frankly with this question, I must concede that a singular case, confirming the truth of this remark, has recently come to my knowledge. A junior member of a leading law

as those who do not. If however, Judge COOLEY disavows any personal knowledge, then his violent invective is entitled to no weight as evidential proof, and must be relegated with his other conceits to the limbo of all visionary hypotheses.

Lawyers, like other professional and commercial men, early acquire distinctive reputations for the leading characteristics they develope. If they habitually overcharge their clients, they soon become known in the community for this trait as well as others. And the great majority of persons desiring to retain an attorney, make the selection after a cautious canvass of all his peculiarities, this among the rest. The client is not confined to a

---

firm in a neighboring city (of which the seniors were and are pre-eminent for personal probity), who had shown a marked preference in his practice for contingent fees, suddenly developed an astonishing propensity " to antagonize the interests of his clients." He rapidly outgrew *in toto* the percentage system. His conception of a contingency culminated in claiming the whole or nothing. Nor was he at all particular about limiting his operations to his own clientage. He was strictly impartial and even generous in the selection of victims—clients, dear friends, members of the bar, aye, even judges and his own partners—very few escaped. But the sequel to this career, so far from supporting, directly overturns Judge COOLEY's position. The man failed utterly at the bar, and was obliged to find more congenial employment elsewhere. The interesting and peculiar phase, however, consists in the upshot of the affair. He is now a self-constituted censor of the profession, and is keenly sensitive to the slightest violation of professional duty and decorum!

single attorney, but may take his choice from a
dozen or a hundred within his reach. If one, therefore, is exorbitant or unreasonable, he may try
another. The lawyer, like those in other callings,
is surrounded by needy men and ambitious rivals,
and if his charges are excessive he will shortly find
himself ignored by those in search of professional
assistance. The average client is quite as able and
willing as the lawyer can be to drive an advantage-
ous bargain, and as they are equally dependant on
each other for service and support respectively,
this question of professional compensation may be
safely left, like the wages of other employés,* to
regulate itself according to the law of demand and
supply. Competition in this as in every other
branch of industry, is after all the surest protection
against injustice or oppression. All this is trite
enough, and is the necessary sequence of the funda-
mental fact in our political fabric, that the lawyer
is merely a citizen like his fellows following a
special vocation. The moral aspect of his claim to
remuneration, including its nature and extent,
hinges on this principle,—that the attorney and

* The New York Court of Appeals have recently held that so
eminent a lawyer as ex-U. S. Attorney General Black, acting in
his capacity of counsel for a corporation, was a mere "employé"
with its other laborers. Gurney *v.* Atlantic etc. R. Co., 58
N. Y., 358.

client are equal in every respect, and have the same needs, rights, duties and obligations. If this axiomatic truth were kept steadily in view, there never could arise among us any differences of opinion on the subject. Indeed, all this platitude and clamor about the danger of lawyers overreaching their clients, are based on the exploded doctrine, that the legal profession is a superior caste, invested with special powers as guardians and protectors of the rest of the community, possessing exclusive rights and privileges, including those of usurping public honors and pilfering public funds; in consideration whereof they are to render their professional services nominally without reward, but really for such private largesses, so called, as by virtue of their greater power and larger experience in their loftier sphere, they can cajole their clients to confer upon them !

But after the relation of attorney and client has been contracted, as in other relations of trust and confidence, all further negotiations and arrangements between them are rightly viewed with suspicion. Before the retainer is accepted the parties are dealing at arms length, each in his own behalf. But after the service has commenced, and the lawyer, entrusted with his client's secrets and interests, has assumed to represent him faithfully, he holds an advantage which the law, as in the case of an agent or trustee, will not permit him to use to the prejudice of his principal. He is then bound to devote his time and talents in the controversy to the exclusive benefit of his employer, and the burden is imposed upon him of proving *uberrima fides* in all his dealings with the client while the relation continues.* Nor is it material whether the arrangement relates to a certain or a contingent fee.† A

---

* Nesbit *v.* Lockman' 34 N. Y., 167; Zeigler *v.* Hughes, 55 Ill., 288; Goodenough *v.* Spencer, 2 Thom. & Cook (N. Y.), 508; Savery *v.* King, 5 House of Lords Cases, 627; Payne *v.* Avery, 21 Mich., 524; Downing *v.* Major, 2 Dana (Ky.), 228.

† A singular case of confusion of thought on this subject is apparent in one of the anonymous " opinions " published in the Law Journal. The writer says: "The most serious objection to it (the habit of receiving contingent fees), as seems to me, is that the lawyer is dealing with his client at an advantage. * * * In a case where I was fairly called upon to work on shares, I declined to name a share, and referred that to two competent friends of the client who were well advised of the nature of the risk. I am by no means sure that all such bargains should not be made invalid, and for this reason alone." If, in the case referred to, the writer was acting as the attorney at the time of the arrangement, his reference to outsiders " to name the share " was only a prudent precaution on his part to secure a valid interest, and the same caution would have been advisable if the fee had been absolute. But if he was not then acting as attorney, the reference was unnecessary and could not affect or mitigate the immorality of his arrangement. If Judge COOLEY'S argument is sound, he was " antagonizing his client" and receiving a corrupt bribe by taking a contingent interest in the suit. The only object of the reference, then, must have been to enlighten his judgment as to the size of his share! But is this writer confident that his client's interests

lawyer who would deceive his client during the litigation for a contingent interest, would be quite as likely to wheedle from him an unconditional fee; and the policy of the law is to prevent all efforts of this character.

Another most remarkable misconception vitiates Judge COOLEY'S reasoning on this topic. He does not hesitate to assume that all of the large and exorbitant fees received in the profession, are necessarily contingent! His favorite illustration involves the amazing assumption that the lawyer who earns only $500 in recovering $20,000 worth of property for his client, will charge precisely that amount if the payment is unconditional, while he will claim $10,000 as a contingent fee! Is it surprising that a grave and experienced judge should, in this manner, reach the most astonishing conclusions? It is a fact, notorious at the bar, that the largest fees are not contingent; and the most extravagant and excessive charges are made by blatant devotees of the old professional "traditions."* As it might

would not have been equally subserved in other cases where he received unconditional fees, if it had been referred to disinterested parties to name the amounts?

* If Judge COOLEY imagines even $10,000 to be an extraordinary fee, let him consult ex-Judge DILLON, his associate in the editorial commission, who will doubtless be able to give him some startling intelligence on the subject. It is stated in the New York Tribune

be deemed invidious to refer to particular cases
which have never been published, although the
subject of common remark at the bar, I will confine myself to instances of unconditional fees
reported in the Law Journal—an authority which
Judge COOLEY, at least, is estopped from questioning. It will appear from the list appended in
a note,* that the Erie Railway Company expended

---

of September 29, 1881, on the authority of Cyrus W. Field, that
the Manhattan Railway Company paid out $43,013,55 "in the first
fourteen days of July" last, "as lawyers' fees" And in The
Nation of October, 6, 1881, it is stated on the same authority, that
the "legal expenses" of this company, in June, "amounted to
over $23,000," "and in the preceding year to $150,000."

* "The following list of counsel fees paid by the Erie Railroad
Company may be of interest. It is taken from a sworn statement
made by the President, Mr. Jay Gould in the action of Thompson
v. The Erie Rrilroad:

Eaton & Taylor ....................................... $39.998 30
D. D. & D. Field ...................................... 31,289 10
David Dudley Field..................................... 12,000 00
Field & Shearman...................................... 5,000 00
William M. Evarts..................................... 15,000 00
C. A. Seward.......................................... 24,000 00
E. W. Stoughton ...................................... 15,500 00
John K. Porter ....................................... 22,000 00
William Fullerton .................................... 11,000 00
John E Burrill........................................ 21,000 00
James T. Brady ....................................... 6,000 00
A. J. Vanderpoel ..................................... 10,000 00
Brown Hall & Vanderpoel .............................. 1,000 00
Edwards Pierpont ..................................... 30,000 00
Martin & Smith........................................ 12,500 00

in a very brief period, for counsel, in one branch of the celebrated Gould and Fisk litigations, the notable sum of $330,510.70. This immense expenditure was duly distributed among the leading lawyers of New York and New Jersey, several firms receiving respectively amounts varying from $15,000 to $48,000. In the Forrest divorce case Charles O'Conor, who certainly did not intend to be exorbitant, re-

| | |
|---|---:|
| J. C. Bancroft Davis | 10,612 00 |
| Levi Underwood | 11,602 00 |
| John Ganson | 15,000 00 |
| Ganson & Smith | 2,031 50 |
| C. N. Potter | 7,000 00 |
| Dimmick & Whitney | 5,000 00 |
| J. N. Whiting | 2,500 00 |
| William H. Morgan | 2,177 80 |
| Cortlandt Parker | 3,100 00 |
| Peter Cagger | 2,000 00 |
| Samuel Hand | 1,000 00 |
| L. Seymour | 1,250 00 |
| J. Bosworth | 1,000 00 |
| Chapman & Martin | 1,000 00 |
| Isaac W. Scudder | 1,000 00 |
| John Hopper | 1,500 00 |
| —— Devlin | 1,000 00 |
| —— Lane | 1,000 00 |
| H. Harris | 1,000 00 |
| Lyman Tremain | 700 00 |
| Rumsey Jones & Roble | 750 00 |
| David Rumsey | 500 00 |
| Bradley & Kendall | 500 00 |
| Spencer Thompson & Mills | 500 00 |
| L. Zabriskie | 500 00 |

See 3 Albany Law Journal, 158

ceived $40,000 from the plaintiff for his services.*
It is stated by the same authority that Sergeant
Wilde received a retainer of 4,000 guineas in the
case of *Atwood* v. *Small*,† saying nothing of "refreshers" and the final settlement.‡ Sergeant Bal-
antine also received a retainer of 5,000 guineas a
few years since, followed by 5,000 more for a service
requiring his presence in India during a period of
three months.§ The great professional fortunes are
coined by corporation attorneys, who thrive on unconditional fees, payable quarterly, on presentation
of bills. If Judge COOLEY has such an intense
aversion to lawyers who deem it proper to look after
their personal and pecuniary interests, why is it
that he reserves all his resentment for those who
accept contingent fees?

But I maintain that it is the duty of the lawyer,
founded on the soundest principles of ethics, to
contract a habit of thrift, and to endeavor to make
his fortune at the bar. He must live like other
men. He must pay his debts and expenses. With
due deference to these philanthropists, his highest
duties are owing to himself, his family and next of

---

* 13 Albany Law Journal, 259.
† 6 Clarke & Fin., 232.
‡ 11 Albany Law Journal, 118.
§ 11 Albany Law Journal, 118.

kin. These he must support and educate, and aim
to leave after him with an estate sufficient to enable
them to buffet "the storms of fate." Besides, it is
the best criterion, and is usually applied by those
wishing to employ a lawyer, that one who will not
protect his own interests is an unsafe guardian of
the interests of others. He must devote himself
exclusively to his profession. He cannot rise to
eminence, nor perform successfully his duty to his
clients, unless he gives his life to its pursuit. To
encourage and enable him to do this, it must yield
all his pecuniary treasures. It must be the solitary
source of his personal fortune as well as his professional fame.

Does not Judge COOLEY recognize this rule in his
own case? The State pays him a yearly salary for
his judicial services. This compensation is supposed to be sufficient to remunerate him for all of
his time during the year. But by dint of special
exertion he is able to detach certain intervals from
his official duties, which he devotes to his professor-
ship and to writing treatises on various branches of
jurisprudence. Should he not regard this extra service as an incident to his judicial office? He is a
"minister of justice," and therefore owes important duties to the profession and the State. Should
he make the performance of these duties redound

to his personal profit? When he is paid for his
time by the State, ought he to accept additional remuneration from a public institution like the University or Law School, or from the publishers of
his books written for the instruction of the profession and the promotion of the principles of justice?
Is it possible that there is any latent motive of a
pecuniary or selfish character which induces him to
perform this extra labor? Does he retain a contingent interest in any of his publications? Does he
ever "subordinate to his personal interests" in
these private speculations the strict performance of
his judicial duties? It might be difficult on his own
principles to give satisfactory answers to all of these
questions. But I am quite willing to relieve him
from any such embarrassment, by conceding that
there is no reason to doubt his moral right to acquire, if he can, a handsome fortune from these additional sources of private professional adventure, so
long as he performs his judicial duties with alacrity
and promptitude. It is only just and right that
persons who devote their lives to particular departments of service, should be able to make them re-
munerative to themselves as well as profitable to the
public.

It is hardly necessary to add that this view of the
lawyer's rights and duties does not imply that he

should descend to the arts of the sharper, either to obtain business or in dealing with his clients. Nor is there any truth in the charge that it has a tendency to increase these practices in the profession. Professional knaves do not tie themselves to any particular routine to effect their purposes. They resort, in turn, to all the methods least likely to acouse the suspicions of their intended victims. But they rarely succeed, in the long run, in gaining wealth or honor. Instead of increasing an income of $5,000 to $20,000, such a practitioner is sure to be driven from the profession to pose, perhaps, as a "high-toned" professor, or editor, or moral lecturer.*

"Touting" does not save him in such an emergency. This has been the last resort of unsuccessful lawyers from time immemorial. It prevails quite as extensively in England as in this country, and is not confined to any particular class of practitioners.†

---

\* Queries: Is the rapacious editor on the scent of new prey ? Having taken his degree as a private in the profession, does he now aspire to partake of public plunder ? Does he imagine that he can practice his impositions on all of the judges ? Will his present pretensions hide from view his past career ? What is the real significance of his sudden and affected conversion ?

† As the editor has published a single specimen of contingent touting, I will offset it by another of the unconditional sort, taken from the Law Journal, vol. 15, p. 16: "Our English brethren are given to criticizing the methods adopted by the profession in this

"Counsel are to be found (says the Pall Mall Gazette) who sign briefs marked with guineas when they receive only shillings, and who take a number of briefs positively at so much a dozen. As for legal touting, that is an old breach of the proprieties, and we are sorry to hear that the practice is an

country to procure business, but we doubt if any advertisement that has appeared on this side of the Atlantic will outdo this circular, issued by a London solicitor: 'I have much pleasure in informing you that I have entered upon a profession for which I was orignally educated; and having been duly admitted upon the roll of solicitors, I have commenced practice at the above address. With a view of becoming more thoroughly acquainted with the theory of the law, I matriculated at King's College, and, having successfully passed the regular examinations, I have been enrolled an associate of that institutien. During my course of study, I had the pleasure in taking the first prize in Professor Leon Levi's class for commercial law, and also Professor Cutler's prize for general jurisprudence. While serving my articles and managing an extensive city practice, I found my commercial knowledge and experience of most essential value. My late principal, in wishing me success, has, in the kindest manner, testified to the tact and skill which I have shown in conducting many varied and important matters in his office. I enclose my card and remain!' "

But even the regenerate editor does not seem to be above giving encouragement to "touters" for a consideration. I observe among several cards, now being published in the Law Journal, one advertising as "attorney and counsel in railway litigations!" And I remember reading in a Schoharie newspaper, shortly after coming to the bar, a long advertisement from a lawyer of the old school, who had just retired from the office of county judge and surrogate and resumed the practice of his profession, in which he gave a list of his charges for all conceivable legal services, from the drawing of a contract to the trial of a cause. He was decidedly definite and certain in his terms of service.

increasing one.''* The special efforts, therefore, to connect these questionable devices with the practice of receiving contingent fees, is quite of a piece with the whole demonstration on this subject, so artfully contrived by the editor and so ingenuously executed by his commission.

Finally, the theory or method of discrimination on which this rule of etiquette is founded, is a plain perversion of the first principles of ethics. It assumes that there is intrinsically something, either good or bad, in a given act, apart from the motive or circumstances of its performance. It transfers the test by which to determine the quality of human conduct from the animus of the actor to the nature of the act itself, tincturing the latter with the elements of virtue and vice instead of holding the person as such to his strict accountability. But it is a proposition too plain for discussion, that the same

---

* 4 Albany Law Journal, 290. At a later date the Law Journal seems inclined to indorse touting to a limited extent. "Dr. Johnson was a moralist, an Englishman, and a man who is usually credited with having possessed an unusual amount of common sense, and it was his opinion that it was proper enough for a lawyer to advertise himself or 'tout' for business, and we have usually found his opinion good enough for us. One thing is certain notwithstanding the 'dignity' and the 'traditions' of the profession, it is better to tout than to steal or to starve, and English barristers have done both the latter within a little time." 13 Albany Law Journal, 360.

act may be commendable and praiseworthy or utterly indefensible, according to the motive or incentive to its performance. Even in the case of homicide the act may be murder or manslaughter, or it may be capable of complete justification in necessary self-defence or the defence of others. The fact, therefore, that a lawyer accepts a contingent retainer, or several of them, does not determine the question of his moral integrity. The particular line or department of business into which he may be thrown is generally governed by circumstances beyond his control. The great body of the profession cannot hope to secure retainers from corporations or the wealthier citizens. While there is usually a considerable variety in the clientage and kind of work required of the lawyer, he is frequently drawn, especially in cities, into some particular department of professional service. In pursuing his specialty he may never have occasion to receive or to reject a contingent retainer, and he may have numerous applications of this character. He may, of course, in either event, be guilty of grossly unprofessional conduct, or he may be, as he usually is, strictly honest and honorable in all his proceedings.

This theory also attempts to limit the application of moral laws, and to substitute for the general

6

code of the whole community the system of a particular class or profession.   Assuming that a set or
collection of persons associated together, or merely
interested in a common purpose, may properly im-
pose arbitrary rules for their own guidance in their
relations to each other, these rules ought not and
cannot control their relations with others outside of
the association.   The client cannot be bound by any
special code of professional ethics which contra-
venes the general rules of society at large.   He is
entitled, in his dealings with every other member
of society, including lawyers as well as physicians
and clergymen, to pursue the methods recognized
in the community as legitimate.   He is under no
greater obligation to trust solely to the honor of his
advocate, than to the honor of a merchant, manu-
facturer or mechanic.   He has the same right to require a written memorandum of the terms of the
agreement with his attorney, as with his carpenter
who undertakes to build him a house, or with his
tenant to whom he leases a habitation.   The policy
of the law is to encourage the making of written
contracts in all business transactions, in order to
prevent subsequent misunderstandings which usually result in litigation.   Ought the lawyer to be re-
lieved from the operation of a general rule which is
deemed of public benefit and utility ?   To claim the

affirmative is to assume that he is superior in this respect to other citizens.

But if such an exception could be properly recognized, other professions would claim the same privileges, and thus the singular anomaly would obtain footing in a republic, that the general rules of the community should yield to the special privileges of each class or profession. Other trades and occupations would also demand similar favors, and we should soon find ourselves retrograding from the principle of uniformity in rights and obligations, towards which mankind have been struggling with varying success for ages. back to the medieval methods of endless complication and diversity—each class, trade or profession having its own peculiar usages and customs for its control and governance. If there is any principle firmly and irrevocably established in modern society, it is this: that the rules of morality are instituted with the consent and for the benefit, and are enforced by the authority, of the whole community.

# ADDRESS.

*Young Gentlemen :*

It has been allotted to me to offer you a few parting suggestions touching the new relation you are about to assume, as you go forth from this graduating class to become members of the legal profession. Putting on your armor for the warfare of life, you will now emerge from the cloisters of preparation for service, to enter the lists of active competition for the prizes and distinctions to which you aspire. You are too earnest and resolute in your devotion to the duties of the profession, to require special incentives to press forward in the career you have chosen. And I feel assured, with the advantages you have enjoyed in this institution, that you are too familiar with the rules of honor and etiquette at the bar, to need advice or admonition concerning the usual restraints of our conventional decorum. I shall therefore spend no time in observations of this character, but hasten directly to the discussion of a practical topic of professional ethics—a question that will unavoidably meet each one of you at

the threshold, and will attend you at every step of
your practice at the bar.    I will also venture the remark that the subject itself, whatever you may
think of the treatment it receives, however strange
and unusual it may appear to the profane public as
a theme for serious consideration on such an occasion, is one in which you, in common with the profession at large, feel a deep and abiding interest.
It involves the reputation of the bar for integrity
and good faith, in following a custom which has become universal in this country—I allude to the practice of entering into personal contracts for professional services.    There is no longer a question of
the legal efficacy of these agreements.    But as the
objection is occasionally pressed with apparent sincerity, that such contracts are opposed to sound policy and good morals, it is important to examine and
answer the objection; or, if this cannot be done, to
discountenance and discontinue the practice.    With
your permission I will, therefore, proceed to consider
briefly the ethics of compensation for professional
services.

Is the lawyer really entitled to any fee or reward
for his services?  If he has this right, what is the
proper measure of his remuneration?  Should it be
the subject of arbitrary regulation by law, or be left
to the mutual arrangement of the parties?  Should

one of the parties, the attorney or the client, have the exclusive power of determining the amount of such recompense?

To the layman of this generation, whose mind is free from the influence of professional caste and the technical subtleties it engenders, the answers to all of these questions would seem to be too obvious for discussion. To him. there would be no limit to the application of the rule, that the laborer is worthy of his hire—and that the terms of service should be determined by mutual consent of the parties in interest. To his mind, the purchaser of manual or mental labor should have the right, in his discretion, to employ additional laborers as the work progressed, without subjecting himself to the complaints or criticisms of those who had borne the heat and burden of the service, so long as all of them received the various sums stipulated in their engagements. In professional as in other employments, each of the parties is equally interested in the performance of the obligations incurred by forming the relation—service by one and payment by the other. Each should therefore have an equal voice in its creation, and in arranging the terms by which it must be controlled. Upon the assumption that all are equal before the law, without regard to wealth, or intelligence, or social or

official station, the relation of employer and employé cannot exist without mutual consent, and
therefore without an explicit understanding concerning the continuance of the service and the limit
of the remuneration. And such, in modern society,
is the invariable rule regulating the rights of parties to all other civil relations of a business character. It is not readily perceived why any distinction
should exist for the particular relation of attorney
and client. There is nothing so peculiar in the
origin or nature of this relation, that it cannot be
properly classified under some acknowledged head
of legal jurisdiction and social order. It is simply
one of the ordinary departments of the law of
agency—one of the familiar sub-divisions of civil
or domestic employment. It does not originate in
any legal or political status of the parties, nor is it
created by any exertion of superior power in the
State. It is a purely voluntary relation of employment or labor, and, like all other relations of this
character, is merely the result of mutual contract
between the parties, involving the obligations of
service on one side and of compensation on the
other. Both parties are therefore subject to the
same rules of law and the same principles of morality that regulate and control all other consensual
relations.

What are these ethical rules and principles? They are all embodied and expressed in the golden precept: "Whatsoever ye would that men should do to you, do ye even so to them." They have their foundation in the original and immutable moral elements of truth and justice. They require of both parties perfect good faith, implicit confidence, fair dealing, honest performance. In the particular relation of attorney and client, the lawyer is obliged to subordinate his views and interests to those of his client; he must exercise all his faculties and powers and resort to all expedient and proper means to preserve and protect the rights he is deputed to represent. He must tell his client the whole truth as frankly when he is wrong as when he is right. He must never advise or encourage, or consent to engage in, a litigation which he is satisfied is without any basis in reason or fact. He is under the highest obligations not to mislead suitors, and not to assist them in perverting legal rules and remedies. He must encounter without fear or favor, and overcome, if possible, all difficulties that retard or prevent the attainment of what he conceives to be his client's rights, but he has no moral or legal commission to lend assistance to a cause which he knows or believes to be dishonest or unjust.

If, then, the lawyer is subject to the same obligations and rules of honor that bind and restrain
others, what principle of public or private morality
requires that any special restriction should be imposed upon him, in the exercise of the absolute
right of parties to make their own contracts.
Doubtless in former times and in other countries,
such restrictions were deemed necessary in nearly
all the departments of social life and industry.
But these restrictions were generally founded on
the theory of class interests and distinctions, which
have no recognition or existence with us. We
legislate not for or against the interests of any
particular class, but for the general good of the
whole community. The only units we recognize in
our society are individuals. All the rules we acknowledge or require for our guidance have reference to the action of individuals. Wherever, in the
private affairs of individuals, there is deception on
one side and delusion on the other, affecting a
substantial right or interest, the law should intervene to prevent the consummation of fraud—but
this rule should be, as it is with us, of universal
application. On the other hand, if the parties have
been honorable and honest in their negotations, and
the final consent was voluntary and mutual, there is
no conceivable rule of ethics, by which the same

terms of service can be regarded as just and right in the contracts of ministers, merchants and mechanics, and wrong or immoral only between attorneys and their clients. The advocate has no peculiar privileges, and ought not to be subjected to any unusual burdens or be deprived of any of the immunities of citizenship. And his right to contract for compensation for his services is as clear in the forum of conscience as that of any other citizen.

He may then with perfect propriety agree in advance on the terms of his advocacy, or leave the question of fees for mutual adjustment after the services have been rendered. He may require prepayment in whole or in part, or special security for subsequent payment, or he may stipulate for contingent compensation out of the proceeds of the litigation. He may, of course, perform his services, relying on the liberality and justice of his client for such remuneration as he deems suitable and proper. And he may, as he always should without hesitation whenever the cause is just and the client is unable to reward him, freely give his services in the interests of benevolence and charity. In other words, he is amenable to the same rules of conduct and subject to the same limitations of honor and decorum that regulate and control the affairs of men in other callings and professions. The

lawyer in real life, like the scientist in material
nature, is exclusively engaged with the facts of
experience.   His time is devoted to incessant efforts
to ascertain the "bottom facts" of all transactions
which are the subjects of controversy between man
and man.   His ceaseless inquiry to all retailers of
whims, notions, opinions, ideas, sentiments and
beliefs, is,—what are the facts?   He, then, above all
others, is bound to recognise facts and to conform
his theories to facts.   He is totally unfitted by the
tendencies of his daily duties and the bias of professional instinct, to profess one thing and practice
another—to live and thrive by dissimulation and
cant.   If his services are required and rendered for
purposes of charity or of gratitude, let him refuse
to receive any reward—let him not under the spe-
cious pretence of receiving a present be fully re-
munerated for an act of friendship or benevolence.

But special objections are sometimes urged against
the common practice of receiving contingent compensation, and it is quite important to ascertain
whether this particular class of contracts should
form an exception to the general rule.   If these
conditional contracts be opposed to the moral sense
or to public policy, they ought not to meet with our
acceptance or approval.   Let us pause a moment on
this particular phase of the controversy.   Perhaps

the fairest method of testing the moral aspects of
this usage is, to compare it with the opposite standard to which it is insisted we ought to conform.
The theory of the *honorarium* requires the advocate to render his services without any formal contract which he can enforce in a legal proceeding,
and to rely on the liberality of his client for such a
reward as he may feel inclined to bestow. It will
be perceived that this method implies that the lawyer performs his service in anticipation of some re-
quital, but the amount is left to the client's sense
of justice and gratitude. Now, if it be proper to
perform the duties of advocacy, with the hope of reward contingent on the will of the client and the
degree of satisfaction with which he receives the
service, it is difficult to detect the impropriety of
making the remuneration contingent upon the
measure of final success. If the advocate can be
induced to overstep the bounds of propriety in
pressing the claims of his clients before the tribunals, he would be more likely to do so under the
spur of an enraged, avaricious or litigious client,
where his douceur depended upon his ability and
inclination to gratify that client's greed and passion,
than where his fee was fixed beyond the power of
the client, and contingent only on the event of the
suit.

The client is often too readily convinced that he only is the aggrieved person in a given controversy, and is frequently more eager for personal success than for impartial justice. In the heat of hostility he will urge his advocate to desperate expedients, by holding out to him promises of liberal reward as the prize of victory. One of the most delicate and difficult duties of the lawyer is, to moderate the exorbitant pretensions of his own client, while striving to defeat the equally unreasonable claims of his adversary. Is he not in a much better position to perform this duty with efficiency, where he is independent of his client's humors— where he knows that his compensation is a matter of right, and not contingent on the variable and irresponsible will of a disappointed litigant? The defeated party can rarely be convinced that he was rightly beaten, and he is predisposed to attribute his misfortune to some mistake or oversight of his own attorney or to the illegitimate methods of the opposite counsel, which he imagines ought to have been foreseen and prevented. Clearly under such circumstances he would not be in a proper frame of mind to fairly appreciate the services of his advocate, and the remuneration he would offer would be neither generous nor just. The lawyer would remain in continual duress, lest his client should sus-

pect him of lukewarmness, and refuse to recognize
any proper claim for remuneration. He would be
subject to the pressing temptation of resorting to
extra-professional methods to secure success, in order to satisfy his client's demands and to obtain his
reward. The client is naturally disposed to guage
the merits of his lawyer by the zeal he manifests
and the result of his efforts. He is under no restraints of professional pride and decorum, which
govern the advocate when he is left at liberty to follow his own judgment in the management of the
cause. There is, I conceive, no greater misconception possible than the theory of the *honorarium*,
which would render the lawyer wholly dependent
on the will of his client. Indeed, it was under the
delusion of this antiquated theory, that the atrocious doctrine was proclaimed by an eminent barrister, afterwards Lord Chancellor of England, "that
an advocate, by the sacred duty which he owes his
client, knows, in the discharge of that office, but
one person in the world, that client, and none other.
To save that client by all expedient means, to protect that client at all hazards and cost to all others,
and, amongst others, to himself, is the highest and
most unquestioned of his duties; and he must not
regard the alarm, the suffering. the torment, the destruction, which he may bring upon any other."

We have, I trust, long since abandoned, with the honorarium, such violent views of professional honor and duty.

But cases frequently occur where contingent compensation is not only proper, but may be indispensable to accomplish the purposes of justice, unless the doctrine be accepted that a lawyer is bound to labor as a bondman for any client who may choose to demand his services. The client may have a just claim, and be utterly unable to advance or to secure a fee except from the subject or proceeds of the litigation. He may be willing to agree that his attorney shall be paid from these proceeds. Is the attorney compelled to reject this fair proposal and to turn him away without redress, because he cannot furnish or secure an unconditional reward? No one, I think, who would concede that legal services are the proper subject of remuneration under any circumstances, would question the right of the lawyer, who had conducted a serious litigation for a poor client to a successful issue without a preliminary contract, to insist upon receiving a proper compensation at the close out of the proceeds of his services, and enforcing it by law. And this is clearly the only alternative he could adopt. But where is the ethical distinction between such a course of proceeding and a contract at the outset, for the same remuneration? In either view the recompense is contingent upon the result, as the client has nothing to pay unless he succeeds, and the attorney performs the service with the expectation of reward depending on this contingency.

But I do not limit the right to agree for a contingent fee to dealings between attorneys and their indigent clients. It extends to every case were the lawyer is at liberty to make any agreement whatever—to every case which he is satisfied is just and honest. The client may desire, by proposing terms of payment wholly or partially contingent on success, to test the sincerity and confidence of the attorney in his own opinion. If the attorney be content to accept such a proposal for a reasonable fee, where is the principle that prohibits it, which would not also prevent any preliminary contract for his compensation? No intelligent person would presume to question the morality of an arrangement by which the owner and tiller of the soil divide between them the profits of the season, or of a transaction between the farmer and the merchant by which the latter retains his commissions from the proceeds of the sale. Does the lawyer occupy a higher moral plane than the humble farmer or the dealers of the market place? This has sometimes been suggested. Is there indeed one rule of mor-

ality for the guidance of the advocate in his relations to others, and a different rule for the rest of
mankind? Are not all of us equally bound by the
one, eternal, immutable rule of right reason, which,
according to the prince of orators, embraces all na-
tions and exists in all times? If there be but one
rule of morals of universal application, and trades-
men in reference to this rule are honorable in their
dealings, members of the bar cannot well incur a
higher obligation.

There is, however, always an important preliminary question to determine before the lawyer can
entertain a proposition from his client in reference
to fees. He must be convinced that it is a proper
case to prosecute or defend. If the claim or defence be not in his opinion just and honest, he
must decline to receive a retainer, large or small,
present or prospective, absolute or contingent.

I have spoken only of the moral right of the
lawyer to enter into agreements for the remuneration of his services. But there is a proper and an
improper method of exercising an undoubted right
or privilege. The true if not the only proper
course would seem to be, as a rule, to leave the
mode of ascertaining the compensation largely to
the choice of the client. If he is content to allow
the services to be rendered on the implied contract

of paying their reasonable value, the attorney ought not to interpose an objection. But many clients, in dealing with lawyers, as with others, wish to know at the outset the extent of the liability they are incurring, and they have an unquestionable right to inquire and ascertain the amount. A lawyer, who should refuse to entertain such an inquiry, would justly be suspected of some ulterior purpose not in harmony with integrity and fairness. If the client desire to make specific terms for compensation, it is equally the lawyer's right to do that, and it would not comport with a proper appreciation of the "dignity of the robe" to evade his proposal or to evince a disposition to repel his advances. Personal honor or dignity is never enhanced, in the relations of business and social life, by assuming superior rights or by affecting greater virtues or higher motives than the mass of mankind. Stripped indeed of all disguises, the law like other trades and professions, is a calling, a vocation, a business, followed as a livelihood—not a caste or grade in political or social order. Other motives of ambition or influence may, at the outset, concur with, and in exceptional cases, eventually prevail over the principal motive, and change the course of a professional career—but these are not the original or controlling incentives with the great mass of

aspirants, who are striving to "climb the steep
where fame's proud temple shines afar."

But the examples of Roman and English history
are often cited in opposition to this view. We are
gravely informed that the only standard of professional honor and decorum is irrevocably settled by
the customs of twenty-five centuries in the famous
forums of ancient Rome and modern England. According to these time-honored precedents, the advocate should receive fees for his service, "not as a
salary or hire but as a mere gratuity, which a counsellor cannot demand without doing wrong to his
reputation;" or as the same rule has been differ-
ently expressed, "the fees of professors of the law
are not duties certain growing due by contract for
labor or service, but gifts, not *merces* but *honorarium.*" I have been careful to state the rule in the
language of eminent jurists and commentators, as it
is recognized in the law of England to-day by the
highest judicial authority.* Merely noting the ob-

---

* The English theory of the honorarium is really a development
of a comparatively recent period. Formerly counsel received retainers directly from their clients, and freely gave them professional advice and assistance without the intervention of attorneys.
The following curious specimen of an agreement between sergeant
and client, made in the year 1501, is preserved by Foss, 5 Lives of
English judges, 21, 22. "This bill indented at London the 16 day
of July, the 16 yeare of the reigne of King Henry the 7th, witnesseth
that John Yaxley, sergent at the law, shall be at the next assises

vious solecism, the contradiction in terms, contained in this definition, that the equivalent received as a reward for services is merely a gift, I pass on to observe, that there were several important limitations to the application of the rule.

1. It did not apply to attorneys or solicitors as distinguished from barristers or advocates. The services of attorneys have always been subject to legal remuneration regulated by a scale of fees covering the various items of service. The successful party in a legal controversy recovered of his adver-

---

to be holden at York, Nottin. and Derb. if they be holden and kept, and their to be of council with Sir Robert Plompton, knight, such assises and actions as the said Sir Robert shall require the said John Yaxley, for the which premisses, as well as for his costs and his labour. John Pulan, Gentleman, bindeth him by these presents to content and pay to the said John Yaxley 40 marcks sterling at the feast of the Nativetie of our Lady next coming, or within eight days next following, with 5 li. paid aforehand, parcell of paiment of the said 40 marcks. Provided alway that if the said John Yaxley have knowledg and warning only to cum to Nott. and Derby, then the said John Yaxley is agread by these presents to take onely xv. li. besides the 5 li. aforesaid. Provided alwies that if the said John Yaxley have knowledg and warning to take no labor in this matter, then he to reteine and hold the said 5 li. resaived for his said good will and labor. In witnesse herof the said John Yaxley, serrant, to the part of this indenture remaining with the said John Pulon have put his seale the day and yeare above written. Provided also that the said Sir Robert Plompton shall beare the charges of the said John Yaxley as well at York as Notingham and Derby, and also to content and pay the said money to the sayd John Yaxley, comed to the said assises att Nott. Derb. and York.

JOHN YAXLEY."

sary under the name of costs for the services of his attorney,* and the defeated party was likewise liable at the same rates to his own solicitor. The fees for services rendered by this subordinate class of lawyers were never regarded as *honoraria*. But with us there is no separation of lawyers into distinct classes, and the services of an attorney and counsellor may be and generally are performed by the same person. There is therefore no reason for any discrimination in relation to the different kinds of professional service. Moreover, it should be noted that the same rule of public policy or morals that would prevent the advocate from enforcing contracts for his compensation, would now apply with greater force to the services of the attorney. In the earlier ages when laws were few and simple, relating only to the most general features of archaic or even medieval society, the principal duties of the lawyer consisted of advocacy in the forum. But in the nineteenth century the rules of legal procedure form the greater part of general legislation, so that it has been not inaptly remarked that the principal

---

* With singular inconsistency the honorarium, given of gratitude by the successful party in a cause to his counsel, may also be taxed and allowed against the opposite party in the final bill of costs. Thus the defeated party, who is under no legal obligation to pay his own barrister, is nevertheless compelled by legal process to repay the "forced gratuities" of his adversary.

object of free institutions is, to get twelve men into the jury box, or to conduct the cause properly through all the preliminary steps of an action at law—and in these greatly altered circumstances, the duties of the attorney comprise the larger share of professional services; he possesses much better facilities than the advocate for stirring up lawsuits and impeding or perverting the course of justice.

2. The *honorarium*, even in its application to the order of barristers, was limited to a particular branch of their regular routine of service, relating strictly to the duties of advocacy. They were at liberty to contract for compensation for any advice or assistance given at their private chambers or beyond the precincts of the court. It has always been a custom in England to retain counsel for this kind of service, either specially or generally by the year, for a stipulated remuneration. An action will lie in favor of the advocate to recover such compensation, while he is unable to enforce payment for any service rendered on the trial of a cause. He may sit in private consultation with the client and attorney and charge for his services, but he can recover nothing for the actual delivery of his argument in open court.

One further fact, however, in this connection will suffice to expose what I must be permitted to characterize as a deliberate deception practiced under cover of this vaunted *honorarium*. It is the invariable usage of the English bar to require prepayment for all services rendered in the line of advocacy. The amount of compensation in the more important cases, is generally arranged between the barrister and the attorney ; and in other cases the attorney usually marks upon the brief the fee he is willing to allow, which the barrister accepts or rejects with the brief at his pleasure. If, in a particular case, the fee be not actually paid to the barrister, it is the duty of the attorney to see that it is secured ; and any solicitor who should neglect to provide for and protect the barrister to whom he intrusted his briefs, would soon lose caste in the profession.*

What then becomes of the claim for the superior honor and dignity of the members of a bar, who devote their lives to their clients from the purest motives of philanthropy ? Practically the client is compelled to pay in advance the amount required by his advocate. The honorary mendicant dictates his own terms to his benevolent employers. And you will readily anticipate the result, verified by

---

* The retaining fee, however, is only supposed to pay for one day's actual service in court. If the trial lasts any longer, it is the duty of the attorney to encourage and stimulate the barrister by daily "refreshers" or additional fees. And these also may be collected from the defeated party.

impartial history, that English barristers have been
from time immemorial the best paid advocates in
christendom. *

---

* There is perhaps no better illustration of the historic halo of
honor, glory and virtue, with which conventionalism and cant
may surround a practice founded in the most intense selfishness
and pharisaism, than that afforded by the English bench and bar
on this subject.  Chief Justice ERLE, speaking for the old court of
Common Pleas in a recent case (Kennedy *v*. Broun, 9 Jur. Rep.
[N. S.], 119) thus enunciates the reason of the rule:  "The incapacity of the advocate in litigation to make a contract of hiring,
affects the integrity and dignity of advocates, and so is in close
relation with the highest of human interests—namely, the administration of justice.  *  *  *  If the law is that the advocate is
incapable of contracting for hire to serve, when he has undertaken
an advocacy, his words and acts ought to be guided by a sense of
duty—that is to say, duty to his client, binding him to exert every
faculty and privilege and power in order that he may maintain
that clients right, together with duty to the court and himself,
binding him to guard against abuse of the powers and privileges intrusted to him by a constant recourse to his own sense of
right.  If an advocate with these qualities stands by the client in
time of his utmost need, regardless alike of popular clamor and
powerful interest, speaking with the boldness which a sense of
duty can alone recommend, we say the service of such an advocate
is beyond all price to the client; and such men are the guarantees
to communities for the maintenance of their dearest rights, and
the words of such men carry a wholesome spirit to all who are
influenced by them.  Such is the system of advocacy intended by
the law, requiring the remuneration to be by gratuity; but if the
law allowed the advocate to make a contract of hiring and service,
it may be that his mind would be lowered, and that his performance would be guided by the words of his contract rather than by
principles of duty; that words sold and delivered according to
contract for the purpose of earning hire would fail to create sympathy and persuasion in proportion as they were suggestive of

Nor, if we go further back, is the Roman precedent more pertinent or efficacious to overthrow our

---

effrontery and selfishness, and that the standard of duty throughout the whole class of advocates might be degraded."

Now what is the practical result of all this "sentimental
nonsense?" The order of barristers protect themselves against
possible loss on their part from the application of the rule,
by requiring prepayment for their services. And on the other
hand they gain all the real benefits to be derived from it, by reliev-
ing themselves from liability for negligence or incapacity in the
performance of their engagements. No action will lie against a
barrister for negligence or even for non-performance of his professional duty. The consequence is, that a barrister of reputation
not only receives enormous fees for services actually rendered, but
numerous retainers for services he never intends to perform. His
contribution box is always open to the reception of all retainers
that may be offered, which he never thinks of returning to the
client; (and no action, of course, will lie to recover back a gift
duly delivered and accepted;) but he selects at the last moment
the most pressing or desirable of half a dozen different engagements, and simply ignores the rest or turns them over to some
starving junior, who is willing to work for the chance of receiving
little or nothing rather than not work at all. It is said that this
practice of "devilling" out their business is one of the sources of
those enormous incomes for which English barristers have become
famous. But there is another still more ludicrous aspect to the
theory or system of "gratuities." Professional etiquette will not
permit a barrister to accept retainers less in amount than the
"fixed scale of fees," nor off from his regular circuit. It is his
duty, therefore, to reject a brief tendered to him under such circumstances. The profession is turned into a trades union to
prohibit barristers from accepting smaller "gratuities" than
custom or etiquette has prescribed. And if a barrister should
attempt to carry out in good faith the vaunted principle of benevolence so eloquently portrayed by Chief Justice ERLE he would
inevitably forfeit his character and position at the bar.

proposition. In Rome the duties of advocacy were an outgrowth of the ancient relation of patron and client, which originated in the political status of the parties,—it was created not by private contract but by the overruling power of public policy. The patron was the protector of his client, who was wholly dependent upon him for the recognition of his rights, either of person or of property. He represented the client's political and civil interests in the State as well as his private rights in the forum. In return, the client was compelled to contribute to the payment of the personal expenses of the patron while engaged in his public duties, as well as the penalties he incurred by the violation of his obligations to the State, and the judgments recovered against him as a burgess in his relations with his peers. The client was also obliged from his private means to assist in raising the sum required for the ransom of his patron as a prisoner of war, and in making up the marriage portions of his daughters; and if the client died without lineal descendants, the patron inherited all of his property. The character of this relation, it is true, was materially modified in the course of centuries, with the growth of the plebeians in wealth, intelligence and power; but it always retained its leading features of influence and protection on one side for dependence and assistance on the other. As, however, with the changes of policy in the government, the more onerous burdens of the clients were removed, the novel practice was gradually introduced of requiring a special reward or *honorarium* for particular services of the patron. To what extent these peculiar presents were the free and voluntary acts of the donors, may be easily conjectured in view of the superior rank and influence of the donees, and the subsequent public enactments on the subject. It would seem that the practice of taking gifts to excess—in polite parlance—became so prevalent as to require the intervention of the Senate to prevent, or, at least, to check the evil. The Cincian law was passed for this purpose, and prohibited in the most stringent terms all gifts or *honoraria* for the services of advocacy.

And even in the latter days of the republic, when the orator had largely assumed the special duties of representing clients in the forum, his relation was not, in any proper sense, akin to that of the modern lawyer to his employers. The orator, as a rule, made no pretension to special or professional knowledge of the laws. In cases of importance requiring particular familiarity with legal rules or knowledge of principles, he applied to a juris-consult for his opinion; and this opinion served as his standard and guide through all the details of the litigation. The orator was really an aspirant for public honors, who merely assumed the role of an advocate in the forum, to ingratiate himself with the populace while he practiced his arts and developed his powers of oratory. He may therefore have been well content to rely upon the personal gratitude of his clients for any immediate remuneration of his services, while he availed himself, without stint or scruple, of their assistance and support to obtain the requisite official preferment to enable him to thrive upon the public treasury.

At a still later period under the empire, when the freedom of speech had been restricted to private controversies in the forum, the orator for the first time betook himself to the law as a study and a profession, and thus developed into the advocate as we now understand his duties and functions. That the Cincian law, however, was not effectual to prevent the continuance of compulsive *honoraria*, is apparent from the adoption of a subsequent law, requiring every suitor to take an oath, before he was permitted to commence an action, that he had not given nor entered into a contract to give anything to his advocate; and this conclusion is still further attested by the Augustan decree, commanding advocates to render their services gratuitously under the penalty of forfeiting four-fold for the benefit of the client. But this policy of absolute prohibition of fees or gifts was finally reversed by the Emperor Claudius, who endeavored to prevent the previous excesses by determining the maximum of *honoraria* which the advocate might lawfully receive, at the sum of ten thousand sesterces. The form of the oath adminis- tered to the suitor at the inception of a cause was also changed, so as to require him to swear that he had not paid, or promised to pay to his advocate, more than the lawful amount. The digest refers in terms to the contracts of advocates for services, and to special securities for their performance on the part of the client, and provides for enforcing in the tribunals such contracts and securities for sums not exceeding the legal maximum. If it be con- ceded that these contracts could only be made after the service had been performed, although the lan- guage of the digest is clearly susceptible of a differ- ent interpretation, still the principle is overthrown on which the *honorarium* is founded, that the advo- cate can, in no event, regard his services as the con- sideration of a contract. But the other construction, that contracts made before the services were ren- dered might also be enforced within the legal limit, is corroborated by a provision of the code, enabling an advocate who had commenced the defense of his client under promise of a definite reward to enforce its payment before the termination of the suit. In any event, it would seem that the restrictions and limitations of the laws were constantly circumvented or ignored; and an effectual means of escape, in an illiterate age, remained ever open to the advocate, in the provision permitting a promise to pay after the service was rendered to be enforced against the client.

But however deeply involved in doubt and difficulty the practice of Roman advocates may be in relation to fees, there seems to be no reasonable cause for dispute that the juris consults, who were the real Roman lawyers, always received compensation for their services, and that their fees were regulated by contracts in the usual manner. The procurators also, who appeared for parties in their causes, performing services similar to those of the modern attorney, were paid for such services, and could enforce contracts for their compensation in the forum.

From this brief retrospect it is apparent that the theory of the *honorarium*, in the light of Roman and English history, is merely a theory and nothing more—a legal fiction which has never been successfully reduced to actual practice. The only result of attempting to enforce this standard of profes-

sional honor in England, has been to inflict upon
clients the additional inconvenience and hardship
of being compelled to pay in advance for the services of an advocate.

Allow me to close with the observation, that if
you are sincere in the mental processes by which
your conclusion is reached, you may adopt either
one of these theories, and perform all your duties
to your clients with honor and fidelity. If the compensation you receive be fair and reasonable in view
of the responsible and difficult task you assume, it
is of comparatively little importance whether it be
present, or prospective, or contingent, or whether the
contract be expressed or implied, so long as the client
lends his sanction and approval. A lawyer may fleece
his clients under any of these methods of procedure,
and subject himself to merited censure, but in every
instance he must be judged by his conduct in the
particular case without reference to his theoretical
standard. "Clear and round dealing is the honor
of man's nature," according to lord Bacon, and it
is indispensible to any permanent success at the
bar. The lawyer may possess the greatest powers
of intellect and the highest inspirations of genius,
he may be profoundly versed in the most abstruse
principles of jurisprudence, he may even explore
the higher realms of philosophy and science, and

penetrating to the furthest confines of human knowledge he may add to these domains new and valuable acquisitions of his own ; but if he is lacking in this essential feature of personal integrity, he will fail, as Bacon failed, in achieving true professional eminence and renown. On the other hand, if he is strong in the assurance of unimpeachable probity and honor, he may be endowed with a far less brilliant intellect, a comparatively cramped and narrow capacity, and he may also labor under the disadvantage of a domineering disposition, a crabbed, censorious, refractory nature ; and yet, with a firm determination to delve into the depths of legal lore, and to discharge his duties to his clients unswerved by the promptings of interest or the allurements of power, he may triumph over all of his competitors, as Coke triumphed over Bacon, and secure the most exalted and enduring professional fame.

# APPENDIX.

[*From the Albany Law Journal, June* 4, 1881.]

At the recent commencement exercises of the Albany Law School, held in this city, an address was made to the graduating class by ex-Judge Countryman, on the Ethics of Compensation as between Attorney and Client. This was an elaborate and ingenious attempt, not simply to justify, but in effect to recommend to lawyers, the practice of taking cases, as Messrs. Dodson & Fogg took Mrs. Bardell's case, on speculation. This is, we dare say, the first public and authoritative apology for this practice ever uttered in this country. Coming from a man of Judge Countryman's recognized position and influence, it must necessarily have weight, and addressed, under the auspices of the law school faculty, to a class of young men just entering on professional life, it may have seemed to bear the approbation of the faculty, and may have sown some mischievous seeds. We cannot believe that the faculty knew beforehand of the tone of the discourse, or that they approved its doctrines and inculcations, which we cannot but regard as pernicious. There can be no doubt that the general and deliberate sense of our profession is against the practice which Judge Countryman justifies. In the few cases which a high-minded lawyer may now and then have undertaken on such terms, he must have done it reluctantly, from force of special circumstances, and with the conviction that it is a custom more honored in the breach than in the observance. Much of Judge Countryman's address was devoted to combating the false delicacy of the idea of the *honorarium*. In this we quite agree with him. The lawyer is worthy of his reward, and he should have the means of compelling payment. The English doctrine on this subject prevails nowhere in this country, we believe, except in New Jersey. Nor do we see any impropriety in a simple preliminary agreement on the amount of compensation, not giving the lawyer an absolute ownership or interest in a cause of action for unliquidated damages. But, says Judge Countryman, there is a large class of cases where poor people—widows and orphans—have claims for damages against powerful corporations, in which large outlay and long delay are necessary to attain justice, and if a lawyer is not permitted to take a pecuniary interest in such cases, how is justice to be done? This is the most plausible and only possibly tenable ground of the argument. If such a case now and then comes to a lawyer, without his seeking it, he may be justified in this course; but the danger is that he will fall into this way, become known and sought by others, and finally be led to seeking such business for himself. Even in this class of cases the theory of the law is that the claimant shall sue *in forma pauperis*, and the court will assign attorneys and counsel who must work without compensation. But when Judge Countryman goes beyond this, and boldly avows the propriety of taking commercial cases, from clients perfectly able to pay, on shares, we utterly and earnestly dissent from him. Here, too, he becomes immeshed in his own argument, for while he insists that the *honorarium* is absurd—that the lawyer ought to be paid at all hazards—he recommends the lawyer himself to run the hazard, to take cases on an agreement by which he may be called on to waste his time and skill, and render services for which he is not to be paid, although he knows his client is quite able to pay him. To be sure, he says the lawyer must not accept a case unless he is convinced it is right. But as we have before this remarked, the advocate is a poor judge on this point. Advocacy blunts the perceptions and blinds the judgment. When you add to the zeal of advocacy a pecuniary interest dependent on success, you introduce a dangerous element. Here is a temptation to manufacture, supply, or warp evidence, to tamper with juries, to lobby with judges, in order to suit their need. Here is a temptation to seek this class of business, or an inducement for it to seek you. This is at all events making merchandise of the law. The lawyer who makes this his practice becomes a huckster, and after a while gets a huckster's conscience. Judge Countryman asks if there is one standard of morals for commercial men, and another for professional men. We say unhesitatingly there is. What may be quite right

for a mere collecting agent, may be quite wrong for an officer of a court of justice.   When Judge Countryman com-
pares the case in hand to the case of an agreement to work
a farm on shares, he makes no allowance for the sanctities,
the temptations, the dignity of the advocate's office and
position.  ˙We think there can be no question about these
things among the better class of lawyers.   We are especially sorry to see a class of young  law graduates dismissed
from their studies with such an ignoble view of a noble and
conscientious  calling.   There was a disheartening moral
discrepancy between the theoretical views of the enthn-
siastic young valedictorian who spoke on the Lawyer's
Code of Honor, and the practical views of the experienced practitioner who spoke on Professional Ethics.

*Editor of the Albany Law Journal:*

Allow me, at the earliest opportunity, in answer to your intimation of last week, to relieve you and the other members of the "faculty" from all responsibility for any "mischievous seeds" that may have been sown by me at the recent commencement exercises of the Albany Law School. It is quite apparent, I think, from the tenor of your article on the subject, that my address had *not* been submitted before delivery to the faculty, for perusal and correction. Permit me also to dissent from your statement, that I "*recommended* to lawyers the practice of taking cases on speculation." On the contrary I distinctly suggested that the proper course on the part of attorneys was to leave the initiative to clients, in respect to the mode of ascertaining and providing for compensation. I contended merely that there was nothing improper or immoral on the part of the lawyer in accepting a fair proposal from his client for contingent compensation out of the proceeds of the litigation, if he was satisfied that the claim was just and honest.

This is not the proper time to discuss the merits of the controversy. I concede there is something to be said in opposition to the view I have taken, and this you have skillfully summarized in your article. But I cannot omit to notice your extravagant assertion that "this is the *first* public and authoritative apology for this practice ever uttered in this country." I may be wrong in my contention, but I certainly have the company of "great and venerable names" in the profession. I will take the liberty of calling your attention to the case of *Bayard* v. *McLane*, 3 Harr. (Del.) 139. The parties to this action represented the two leading families in the State of Delaware, in culture, character and social worth. James A. Bayard was the acknowledged leader of the local bar, and a senator of the United States, in which position he has been succeeded by two of his sons and a grandson, the present senator of that name. Allen McLane was a distinguished revolutionary officer, and his son Louis, after practicing law a few years, became successively member of Congress, senator, minister to England, secretary of State and of the treasury. In 1812, Allen McLane, while holding the office of United States collector for the district of Delaware, having seized several vessels of Stephen Girard, for violation of the revenue laws, which he claimed as forfeitures, entered into a contract with his son Louis and Mr. Bayard, by which the two latter were to conduct the litigations through the courts, and were each to receive as compensation contingent on success, one-third of the share allowed by law to the collector from the forfeitures. You will observe that this was not a common case of private right, but a bald speculation all round, with no such alleviating circumstance as you seem to require to justify a "high minded lawyer" in occasionally stooping to receive a contingent fee. Nor was there the slightest "commercial" taint attaching to any of the parties. After the trial of one of the suits, Mr. Bayard was appointed one of the commissioners to negotiate the treaty of Ghent, and died immediately after returning home from his mission, without taking further part in the litigations. In the action to recover on the contract, for his services, the defense was : 1. That the contract was illegal. 2. That it was not performed. It would be difficult to find in the books a case which received more extended and careful consideration. It was argued twice by lawyers of the first rank at the American bar, one of the judges having died after the first argument, lasting thirteen days, which necessitated a reargument, occupying eleven days. The validity and propriety of the agreement was sustained at the bar, among others, by Reverdy Johnson of Baltimore, afterward attorney-general of the United States and senator from Maryland, and Joseph P. Comegys, the present chief justice of Delaware ; and was assailed, among others, by John Sergeant and William M. Meredith of Philadelphia. The members of the court, however, were unanimous in reaching the conclusion as announced by Harrington, J., "that there is nothing in the stipulated service that the law ever prohibited, and nothing in the mode of compensation that violates any principle of law or morals." (P. 217.) Is not this a "public and authoritative apology," if one is needed, for the "pernicious" practice you have censured so severely ?

There are many other authorities of the same character, which I omit for want of space. I will only call attention

to a few recent decisions.   The Supreme Court of Wisconsin overruled the objections of champerty and immorality
to a similar contract, holding that it was too clear for discussion.   The attorneys who made the contract in that
case were Edward G. Ryan, afterward chief justice of the
State, and Matthew H. Carpenter, the brilliant lawyer and
senator, recently deceased.   *Ryan* v. *Martin*, 16 Wis., 59 ;
18 id., 672.   Mr. Justice McArthur, speaking for the Supreme Court of the District of Columbia, in a recent
case, said :  "All agreements made for mere contingent
compensation are generally meritorious, and should be
enforced.   The most respectable counsel conduct immense litigations with no other hope of reward."  *Stanton* v. *Haskin*, 1 McAr., 558. 562.   In another case in
this State, where the attorney went so far as to take a
formal assignment of the claim and prosecuted it in his
own name, for the benefit of the client, under a contract for a contingent fee, the General Term, per Johnson,
J., said :  "There is nothing necessarily immoral or censur-
able in aiding and assisting another in the prosecution and
collection of a just claim, or one which is believed to be
such, by the party assisting, where such assistance is sought
in good faith by the party so assisted.   On the contrary,
such acts from good motives, and for just ends, may be as
commendable and praiseworthy as any other acts of benevolence and kindness."  *Voorhees* v. *Dorr*, 51 Barb., 580,
586.   The United States Supreme Court have recently held,
Chief Justice Waite delivering the opinion, that "there is

nothing illegal, immoral or against public policy, in an agreement by an attorney to prosecute a claim, either at a fixed compensation, or for a reasonable percentage upon the amount recovered " ( *Wright* v. *Tibbitts*, 1 Otto, 252) ; and still later, Clifford, J., speaking for the whole court, said " that the proposition (the propriety of such a contract) is one beyond legitimate controversy." *Stanton* v. *Embrey*, 3 Otto, 556. Does the Law Journal refuse to recognize these high " authorities ?"

Respectfully,

E. COUNTRYMAN.

ALBANY, *June* 6, 1881.

## THE ETHICS OF PROFESSIONAL COMPENSATION.

*[From the Albany Law Journal, June 18, 1881.]*

In his communication to this Journal last week, Judge Countryman says that we were in error in stating that he "recommended" the practice of attorneys being contingently interested in the subject of litigation as a means of compensation ; that he simply vindicated the practice against the charges of immorality and impropriety ; and that he "recomended" that the suggestion should in every case come from the client. Judge Countryman certainly spoke strongly in support of the practice ; but if he does not think this amounts to a "recommendation," we shall not quarrel with him over that word. But he seems to have some instinctive doubt of the propriety of the practice ; else why leave it to the client to make the advance? If the practice is right, this is a false delicacy ; if wrong, the lawyer cannot shield himself by saying, "my client tempted me." A man who unlawfully keeps and sells poison cannot escape by pleading that the customer asked him for it.

Judge Countryman says we are "extravagant" in pronouncing his the first public apology for the practice ever pronounced in this country. We had practitioners in mind in saying that. We should hardly call a judicial expression an "apology" for a practice. But let us see how his judicial authorities stand. The Delaware case is the most elaborate defense of the practice which he cites. Mr. Bayard was undoubtedly a highly respectable man and lawyer, but he lived in a State where there never had been any public sense opposed to the practice. Champerty and maintenance never existed in that State. So he held slaves, we suppose, and thought it right. He took a single claim to collect for a percentage ; it does not appear that he was in the habit of doing this thing. We hardly think his son, the present senator, would advocate such a practice in these days. But what is said on this subject in the Delaware case is *obiter*, after all, for the court held that Mr. Bayard had not performed his part of the contract, and therefore there could be no recovery on it.

In *Voorhies* v. *Dorr*, 51 Barb. 586, the question did not arise and was not discussed. The action was by a layman to recover an agreed compensation for the defendant lawyer's use of the plaintiff's name in a lawsuit, and what the court said was in reference to that contract.

The language which Judge Countryman attributes to Chief Justice Waite, in *Wright* v. *Tebbetts*, 1 Otto, 252, is not the language of the judge, but of the reporter's headnote. All that the judge said on the subject was: *"After the service had been rendered, and after,* as was supposed, *the claim had been secured,* Wright agreed to pay ten per cent of the amount eventually realized, as compensation for the labor done. We see no reason to find fault with this."

The court did use the language quoted from *Stanton* v. *Haskin*, 1 McArthur, 558 ; S. C., 27 Am. Rep. 612. But it was *obiter*. If Judge Countryman had pursued his quotation one sentence, he would have found this : "But in this case there is an effort to recover land, not as a measure of compensation, but as a part of the very property in controversy." And the court refused to enforce the agreement between the attorney and client, by which the former was to have one third of the land recovered.

The Wisconsin cases cited by Judge Countryman, while they pronounce the practice lawful, afford no breath of sanction of the morality or propriety of the practice.

This examination reduces Judge Countryman's array of indorsers to a very small showing. Now let us look at the other side, commencing at home, and coming from the time when the practice was unlawful down to the present time, when it is lawful. Chancellor Kent said, in *Arden* v. *Patterson*, 5 Johns. Ch. 48: "The purchase of a lawsuit by an attorney is champerty in its most odious form ; and it ought equally to be condemned on principles of public policy. It would lead to fraud, oppression, and corruption. As a sworn minister of the courts of justice, the attorney ought not to be permitted to avail himself of the knowledge which he acquires in his professional character, to speculate in lawsuits. The precedent would tend to corrupt the profession, and produce lasting mischief to the community."

The arguments on this side of this question have never

been better presented than by ex-Judge Samuel Hand, of this city, who, in his address as president of the New York State Bar Association, in 1879, after rehearsing the common arguments in favor of the practice, said : "It is urged that practices, which before the Code were universally regarded in the profession as disreputable, unworthy, demoralizing, and tending to degrade the profession and impair the administration of justice, are not changed in their character, because they may possibly have ceased to be illegal, or to be absolutely prohibited by statute ; or because a law removing restraints upon them has been passed at a time when it seemed to be the fashion to throw down every legal barrier to, and restraint upon, the admission of an attorney, or his practice when admitted, and to rely solely upon the diligence, the integrity and honor of men as a sufficient safeguard. It is also urged that the character of these practices remains the same as ever; that they are still, as ever, demoralizing and deteriorating in their tendency ; that they do, as ever, tend to barratry, to stirring up of suits, the encouragement of litigation, and the tampering with evidence. That they are an easy and tempting source of large profits to able and adroit lawyers ; that such cases, with proper management, are sure to succeed before juries, and that it is rare that a case cannot, on some question, be got before a jury ; that the communistic tendencies of the present time produce enormous verdicts—fortunes in themselves ; that such temptations are calculated to drag away the profession from its moorings, and its regular steady business, to these barratrous speculations ; that while there may be no harm in arranging for a contingent fee with a poor man, who applies to an attorney, yet the tendency of permitting such arrangements is to set members of the profession advertising for such cases, soliciting at the expense of all manly and professional dignity, persons who are known to have causes of action, and inducing them to violate constantly the statute against the advancing of moneys as an inducement to placing suits in their hands. It is said that worthless persons, having nothing, risking nothing, are induced under this system to present and swear through simulated causes of action, relying upon attorneys to furnish all necessary moneys and divide the profits if successful. All these mischiefs and irregularities are, it is insisted, injurious to the standing before the world and to the inward tone of the profession."

On the same occasion, Mr. Tracy C. Becker, of Buffalo, in an essay on Contracts for Contingent Compensation for Legal Services, remarked : "I cannot conceive of any serious argument that will convince any one that such speculations are not demoralizing and dangerous in the extreme." "With the frequency of contracts for contingent compensation the money changers and speculators insiduously, yet surely, gain a foothold on the threshold of that noble edifice. Would it not be well to imitate that great law-giver and moralist who, when he found them clinging about another temple two thousand years ago, scrupled not to overturn their tables, and to drive them forth lest their presence should pollute the sacred place?"

Although the practice in question is now lawful in this State, the courts do not seem to regard it with much favor. In *Voorhies* v. *McCartney*, 51 N. Y., 390, the commission of appeals held that an attorney under such circumstances, bringing an action in the name of another, is still liable for the defendant's costs; and Gray, C., observed: "The repeal of the former laws upon that subject has not legalized such contracts; it made such transactions by lawyers only tolerable by leaving such of them as might choose to embark in such enterprises upon the same footing as other speculators, any one of whom may employ an attorney to bring an action in which he is beneficially interested in the name of another."

In *Coughlin* v. *N. Y. C. & H. R. R. R. Co.*, 71 N. Y., 443; S. C., 27 Am. Rep., 75, the court held that in spite of an agreement of the nature in question, the client could release his claim to the defendant and defeat his attorney. The court, Earl, J., remarked: "Its exercise" (*i. e.*, the extraordinary power of the court) "to secure to an attorney the statutory fees, small in amount and easily ascertainable, was just and proper, and could lead to no abuse. But to exercise it so as to enforce all contracts between clients and attorneys, however extraordinary, is quite another thing. Here the attorneys were contractors. They took the job to carry this suit through, and to furnish all the labor and money needed for that purpose, and they are

9

no more entitled to the protection which they now seek than any other person not a lawyer would have been, if he had taken the same contract. When a party has the whole legal and equitable title to a cause of action, public policy and private right are best subserved by permitting him to settle and discharge that, if he desires to, without the intervention of his attorneys."

Now to go outside our own State. In *Duke* v. *Harper,* 66 Mo., 51 ; S. C., 27 Am. Rep., 314, the court said : "But there is nothing in the law of champerty as expounded by Blackstone and Bouvier, and the American courts in the adjudicated cases which we have cited, that is not applicable to our condition. The race of intermeddlers and busybodies is not extinct. It was never confined to Great Britain, and the little band of refugees who landed from the May Flower on the coast of New England were not entirely free from the vice of intermeddling in the concerns of other people. It is as prevalent a vice in the United States as it ever was in England, and we do not see but that a law restraining intermeddlers from stirring up strife and litigation betwixt their neighbors is wholesome and necessary, even in Missouri. A man having a doubtful claim to property in the possession of another, who would hesitate to incur the expense of testing its validity, will readily agree that one who will bear the burden of the contest, and take part of the recovery for his pay, may institute the suit in his name. Such contracts are champertons and should be so held on principle everywhere."

In *Adye* v. *Hanna*, 47 Iowa, 264 ; S. C., 29 Am. Rep. 484, the court held that an attorney's agreement to pay any judgement against his client if he would appeal and pay his fees, is void, and remarked : "In another respect it is in conflict with the policy of the law, which promotes and upholds purity and justice in the administration of remedies in the courts. The attorneys bound by the contract become liable in the place of their client. They have the most powerful motive to pervert justice and corrupt its source, in order to escape the liability they have assumed. They are officers of the court, and as such ought to be trusted by judges as well as clients. Their duty does not require them to pervert the law or deceive those clothed with the power to administer it. On the contrary, it forbids them, under the heaviest penalties, to do any act that may have such an effect. They are to aid the courts in the administration of justice. Their duty requires them to endeavor to secure to their client his rights under the law and nothing more. For such services the law will secure them compensation from their clients. It requires neither arguments nor explanations to show what great temptations would be placed before the attorney to violate his duty and to endeavor to corrupt the fountain of justice, were he to take the place of his client and become responsible for all liabilities incident to a decision adverse to him. The law will not permit members of the legal profession to be assailed with temptations so dangerous in their character. They have the most

grave duties to perform in the administration of justice ;
they stand before the world, as a class, distinguished for
honor, integrity, and public virtue. The law will be careful to recognize no rules or principles which in their application to the practice of courts or business of attorneys
may tend to corrupt the legal profession, or rob it of the
high character it has always maintained."

In Pennsylvania, Chief Justice Gibson characterizes the
practice as "questionable." *Foster* v. *Jack*, 4 Watts, 339.
Judge Rogers says it. is a "subject of regret." Judge
Kane, in *Ex parte Plitt*, 2 Wall. Jr., 452, says : "It is not
a practice to be generally commended."

From Chief Justice Sharswood's admirable essay on
Professional Ethics we extract the following : "A horde
of pettifogging, barratrous, custom-seeking, money-mak-
ing lawyers, is one of the greatest curses with which any
community can be visited." "Except in this class of
cases" (undefended claims) "agreements between counsel
and client that the compensation of the former shall de-
pend upon final success in the lawsuit—in other words, contingent fees—however common such agreements may be,
are of a very dangerous tendency, and to be declined in all
ordinary cases." "It is to be observed, then, that such a
contract changes entirely the relation of counsel to the
cause. It reduces him from his high position as an officer
of the court, and a minister of justice, to that of a party
litigating his own claim. Having now a deep personal interest in the event of the controversy, he will cease to con-

sider himself subject to the ordinary rules of professional conduct. He is tempted to make success, at all hazards and by all means, the sole end of his exertions. He becomes blind to the merits of the case, and would find it difficult to persuade himself, no matter what state of facts might be developed in the progress of the proceedings, as to the true character of the transaction, that it was his duty to retire from it. It places his client and himself in a new and dangerous relation. They are no longer attorney and client, but partners. He has now an interest which gives him a right to speak as principal, not merely to advise as to the law and abide by instructions. It is either unfair to him or unfair to the client. If he thinks the result doubtful, he throws all his time, learning and skill away upon what, in his estimation, is an uncertain chance. If he believes that the result will be success, he receives in this way a higher compensation than he is justly entitled to receive. It is an undue encouragement to litigation. Men who would not think of entering on a lawsuit, if they knew that they must compensate their lawyer whether they win or lose, are ready upon such a contingent agreement to try their chances with any kind of a claim. It makes the law more of a lottery than it is. The worst consequence is yet to be told—its effects upon professional character. It turns lawyers into higglers with their clients. Of course it is not meant that these are always its actual results; but they are its inevitable tendencies—in many instances its practical working. To drive a favorable bargain with the suitor in the first place, the difficulties of the case are magnified and multiplied, and advantage taken of that very confidence which led him to intrust his interests to the protection of the advocate. The parties are necessarily not on an equal footing in making such a bargain. A high sense of honor may prevent counsel from abusing his position and knowledge; but all have not such high and nice sense of honor. If our example goes toward making the practice of agreements for contingent fees general, we assist in placing such temptations in the way of our professional brethren of all degrees—the young, the inexperienced, and the unwary, as well as those whose age and experience has taught them that a lawyer's honor is his brightest jewel, and to be guarded from being sullied, even from the breath of suspicion, with the most sedulous care."

Chief Justice Sharswood, in the same essay, quotes the following advice from Price on Limitation and Lien, characterizing the author a "a gentleman of the largest experience and highest character for integrity and learning at the Philadelphia bar:" "Permit me to advise and earnestly to admonish you, for the preservation of professional honor and integrity, to avoid the temptation of bargaining for fees or shares of any estate or other claim, contingent upon a successful recovery. The practice directly leads to a disturbance of the peace of society, and to an infidelity to the professional obligation promised to the court, in which is implied. an absence of desire or effort, of one in the ministry of the temple of justice, to obtain a success that is not just as well as lawful. It is true, as a just equivalent for many cases honorably advocated and incompetently paid by the poor, a compensation may and will be received, the more liberal because of the ability produced by success; but let it be the result of no bargain, exacted as a price before the service is rendered, but rather the grateful return for benefits already conferred."

If our language on this subject is deemed "severe," what will be said to that of the foregoing extracts? Does our correspondent refuse to recognize these high anthorities?

*Editor of the Albany Law Journal:*

The closing interrogatory of your elaborate article, last week, seems to invite a response. I am not reluctant to accept your summons. My previous communication was merely designed to meet your assumption that there were *no authorities* to sustain the views I had advanced relating to contingent compensation. I promptly gave you a few citations which seem to have required an extra week for thorough digestion. And what is your answer? You suggest, in reference to the Delaware case, that Mr. Bayard was a slaveholder! And you aver that "what is said by the court on this subject is *obiter*," because Mr. B. had not performed his part of the contract. Let us see. The court could not logically reach the question of non-performance until it had affirmed the validity of the contract. If the agreement had been held illegal, it would have been immaterial whether it had been performed or not, and the action would have been dismissed without considering the latter point. In determining the *status* of the contract, the court adjudged that the English statutes of champerty were not recognized in Delaware : and as there was no local statute on the subject, the only remaining proposition involved in the decision was necessarily whether the agreement was tainted with immorality. But I humbly submit that even an *obiter* expression of opinion after solemn argument, by the highest tribunal of a sovereign State, is quite as authoritative as the *ex parte* effusions of the most eminent journalist or practitioner at the bar.

You misinterpret my language in reference to the case in 1 Otto, 252. I did not attribute my quotation to the chief justice, but stated that he delivered the opinion, giving in the same connection the point of the decision in the language of the syllabus, which is a correct abstract of the case. But in the other citation from the same court (*Stanton* v. *Embrey*, 3 Otto, 548), to which you make no allusion, I gave the language of Judge Clifford ; and in that case the contract for contingent remuneration, *if the time* be important, was made *before* any of the services were rendered.

You are equally unfortunate in your criticism of the case from 1 McArthur, 558. The court, while distinctly asserting that the contract was unobjectionable on moral grounds, held it to be illegal merely because it fell within the prohibition of the English statute of champerty, which had always been held to be a part of the common law of Maryland, and therefore of the District of Columbia.

You are correct in stating that the contract in *Voorhies* v. *Dorr*, 51 Barb., 586, was made with a layman, a fact which I had overlooked. But it does not affect the principle in the slightest degree. Judge Johnson said : "The arrangement between the parties, falls *exactly* within the general definition of maintenance." But as the English statute on that subject was adjudged not to be law in this State, and there was nothing immoral in the contract itself,.

it was strictly enforced. The same court had previously applied the same rule to a contract between an attorney and client for a contingent fee. *Benedict* v. *Stuart*, 23 Barb., 420. In the latter case Judge Welles, in delivering the opinion, said: "That part of the bargain—that the plaintiff and Mr. Martindale were to have 20 per cent of the amount to be recovered, which is the only feature of the transaction claimed to be champertous, would, when viewed in connection with the other parts of the agreement, tend to *repress*, rather than promote, a litigation between the defendant and the railroad company." P. 421. And Mr. Martindale has since held the high position of attorney-general of this State.

You finally suggest that "the Wisconsin cases cited, while they pronounce the practice lawful, afford no breath of sanction of the morality or propriety of the practice !" Is it necessary to refer a professor of law to the maxim, *ex turpi contractu, non oritur actio ?*

But I only gave you a few samples from many authorities bearing directly on the point in controversy. I now send you another installment, without note or comment, to which it is time you should devote a little attention : *Major's Ex'rs* v. *Gibson*, 1 Pat. & H. (Va.), 48 ; *Marsh* v. *Holbrook*, 3 Abb. Ct. of App. Dec., 176 ; *Fitch* v. *Gardenier*, 2 id., 153 ; *Schomp* v. *Schenck*, 40 N. J. Law, 195 ; *Hunt* v. *Test*, 8 Ala., 713 ; *Wright* v. *Meek*, 3 Green (Iowa), 472 ; *Martinez* v. *Vines*, 32 La. Ann., 305 ; *Maybie* v. *Raymond*, 15 Nat. Bank. Reg. Rep., 353, 361 ; *Bentick* v.

*Franklin*, 38 Tex., 458, 473 ; *Lytle* v. *The State*, 17 Ark., 608, 670.

You wish to know what I think of the authorities you have cited. Noting your solicitude to escape from the issue you tendered, that there were no authorities sustaining my view ; and your desire now to fall back upon another and distinct issue, whether there are *any* in support of yours, which I never thought of questioning, I follow you with pleasure. You cite seven judicial decisions, only two of which have any application to the point in dispute, and those are two of the strongest authorities I have seen against your position. In *Foster* v. *Jack*, 4 Watts, 334, the action was brought by an attorney to recover the value of his services on an implied assumpsit. There was no express contract either for an absolute or contingent fee. The opinion of Chief Justice Gibson was devoted to an explanation of a former decision in which he had concurred, holding that no action would lie in favor of a lawyer to recover his fees. This decision he now assisted in overruling, maintaining the right of the attorney to his reward. The learned judge remarked : "This is not the time nor the place to discuss the legality of contingent fees ; " and he refused to consider that question.

In *Adye* v. *Hanna*, 47 Iowa, 264, the attorneys, to induce their client to bring an appeal, after a trial at nisi prius, agreed to pay all the costs, if he should be beaten. The court properly held that the contract was void, and used the vigorous language you have quoted. May I ask, why you cited this case? The contract on the part of the attorneys was for an absolute, not a contingent fee, of $27.50 ! P. 265. But you conceded at the outset that such a contract was perfectly proper ! Do you mean then to apply this judicial condemnation to yourself? If it has any application to this controversy, it points directly against your position. The simple fact is, that in this, as in all other cases where similar language is used, the denunciation is directed not against the principle involved in either class of contracts, but against special features of deception or corruption in the particular case.

In *Voorhies* v. *McCartney*, 51 N. Y., 387, the only question was whether the attorney, who was beneficially interested in the claim, and had advised its transfer by a nonresident owner to an insolvent person in the State, for the purpose of bringing the suit, was liable for the costs of the opposite party, under the statute which provides that such person "shall be liable for costs in the same cases, and to the same extent, in which a plaintiff would be liable ;" and it was decided in the affirmative.* The particular remark quoted by you from the opinion of the court, is as unintelligible as it was unnecessary. How a contract "not legalized" is "only tolerable," I leave for you and the learned commissioner to explain.

---

* But the Court of Appeals held the other way under the same statute. Sussdorf *v.* Schmidt, 55 N. Y , 320. And in the late revision the language of the statute was changed to conform to this decision and remove all doubt on the subject. Code of Civil Procedure, § 3247.

The cases of *Arden* v. *Patterson*, 5 Johns. Ch. 44, and *Coughlin* v. *N. Y. C. & H. R. Co.*, 71 N. Y., 443, may be considered together. In the first case, the attorney purchased the entire cause of action and prosecuted it in the name of another ; and in the second, he stipulated "to find all the money necessary to carry on the case." Of course it was held in each suit that the attorney violated the statutes prohibiting the purchase of claims for prosecution, or the advance of money as an inducement to litigation. The language quoted from the chancellor, had no reference whatever to contracts for services, but related to the purchase of claims for the purpose of prosecution. And in the second case, Judge Earl stated the true distinction, with his usual perspicuity. He said : "An attorney may stipulate with his client for any compensation they may agree upon, and such compensation may be absolute or contingent ; but he may not purchase a claim for prosecution, and he may not advance, or agree to advance, any money for the purpose of inducing a party to place a claim in his hands for collection." 71 N. Y., 453. But this very distinction is recognized in the Delaware case and in all the authorities I cited.

In *Duke* v. *Harper*, 66 Mo., 51, the contract of the attorneys was for one-fourth of the claim, contingent on success. Judge Henry vindicated the champerty laws, denouncing "the race of intermeddlers and busy-bodies" as you have stated, and concluded as follows : " The contract under consideration, however, is not champertous, because while the attorneys agreed to receive as a compensation for their services, as such, a portion of the property in controversy, they did not bind themselves to pay any portion of the expenses of the litigation." P. 61. The court below, in reaching the same conclusion (2 Mo., App. 1), uses this language: "We see nothing contrary to the welfare of society and the administration of justice in upholding a contract between attorney and client, that the attorney should be paid out of the thing recovered. On the contrary, many a poor man with a just claim would find himself unable to prosecute his rights, could he make no arrangement to pay his advocate out of the proceeds of the suit. Such contracts have been of constant occurrence throughout this State, and if they are immoral or illegal, there are perhaps few attorneys in active practice amongst us who have not been habitual violators of the law." Pp. 10, 11.

But your crowning citation is *Ex parte Plitt*, 2 Wall. Jr. 452. This is an interesting case. It involved the validity of conflicting claims of many persons as heirs at law to an estate amounting to $800,000. After the suit had been tried at the Federal circuit in Pennsylvania and an appeal had been taken to the Supreme Court of the United States, an arrangement was made with the successful claimants and their attorneys, by which Messrs. Tilghman and Newbold, two eminent lawyers of Philadelphia, and a third lawyer at Washington, to be selected by them, were to take charge of the case in that court, and receive "a commission of $7\frac{1}{2}$ per cent, contingent on the amount recovered "—to " be divided into thrée equal parts, $2\frac{1}{2}$ to Mr. Tilghman, $2\frac{1}{2}$ to Mr. Newbold, and $2\frac{1}{2}$ to the third counsel at Washington." Daniel Webster was afterward selected as the " third counsel," and was informed of the agreement. Mr. Webster (who was opposed to slavery), " pleasantiy asked whether they could not get ʀomething as they went along, ' enough at least to nib the pen?'" On being informed that this was impossible, he assented to the terms and participated in the argument, which resulted in sending the case back for a new trial. The same parties having succeeded again, another appeal was taken to the Supreme Court, where after being twice argued, the judgement was finally affirmed by an equal division of the judges. Mr. Webster took no part in the case after the second appeal. His engagements as secretary of State probably precluded his doing so, on the preliminary argument, and he died before the reargument took place. Messrs. Tilghman and Newbold received the $7\frac{1}{2}$ per cent, \$60,000, for their services, but paid no portion of it to Mr. Webster or to his representatives. His executors, disclaiming any connection on his part with the contract for a contingency, doubtless because as in the Bayard case he had failed to perform, applied to the court for a reasonable allowance out of the fund for his services. And this petition was granted, the court expressly approving of the contract in all its particulars, as reasonable and proper.

> " While we such precedents can boast at home,
> Keep thy Fabricius and thy Cato, Rome!"

These are *your* judicial authorities! If I were inclined
to pursue your peculiar methods of imputation, I might
very properly pause here to inquire whether a "huckster"
would have been justified in wresting the condemnatory
remarks of the judge in the Missouri case from their proper
connection, to give the court the appearance of censuring
a contract which it distinctly approved? And I might also
ask whether "a huckster's conscience" whould have permitted him to misapply the indignant comments of the
court, in the Iowa case, relating to a contract for an absolute fee, which he approved, to an agreement for a contingent fee, which he condemned? But I am too well pleased
with all your citations to wrangle with you over these little
indiscretions. If after another twelve days' search you
should still be unable to produce a single case in support
of your views, I was about to say that I would undertake
to furnish it myself, but I will think of that.

Now a few words with reference to your quotation from
Sharswood's "Legal Ethics," and the deliverances of two
of our local celebrities. As the essay of Judge Sharswood
is the source and inspiration of the other disquisitions, it
will be unnecessary to refer to them in detail. Judge
Sharswood's book is doubtless the ablest presentation of
the honorarium theory in the language. And whatever may
be thought of his arguments, it must be admitted that he
is thoroughly in earnest and consistent in his views. He
gives his unqualified adhesion to the English rule, that it
is wrong and undignified to enter into a preliminary con-

tract for the services of advocacy, but highly honorable to insist on *pre-payment* before the service is rendered! Judge Sharswood objects to any contract between the advocate and client, and your first quotation from his essay is a portion of his criticism on the propriety of such a contract for an absolute, not a contingent fee! His entire review of the subject of compensation is one continuous lamentation over the tendencies of American decisions to abandon the obsolete and fantastic theories of ancient Latium touching the relation of patron and client. I have considered all these topics in my address, and shall not stop to repeat myself here.

But I cannot permit you to take shelter behind Judge Sharswood or any other gentleman. If he is right your views are as untenable as mine. You have constructed a tub for yourself and it must stand on its own bottom. If you have indiscreetly contracted your area it is your affair, and you must take the consequences. Now you have expressly approved that portion of my address "devoted (I quote your language) to combating the false delicacy of the idea of the honorarium." You have conceded in terms that there is "no impropriety in a simple preliminary agreement on the amount of compensation, not giving the lawyer an absolute ownership or interest in a cause of action for unliquidated damages." You also concede that "the lawyer is worthy of his reward, and should have the means of compelling payment." But it is precisely such concessions and the practices they encourage that Judge

10

Sharswood deplores, as tending to create "a horde of pettifogging, barratrous, custom seeking, money making lawyers—one of the greatest curses with which any community can be visited!"

You have further conceded that a "highminded lawyer" may now and then, "under special circumstances," take a "few cases" upon contingencies, and "be justified in this course." This is an admission that there is nothing immoral at least in the practice, to this limited extent. But you are bound to mark the limitation and to draw the line beyond which "the better class of lawyers" may not pass. How many of these cases may one lawyer accept without peril? After having taken one, how long a time must intervene before he can properly accept another? If ten clients having similar cases at the same time wish to employ the same attorney, how many of them must he reject because they happen to come in "a heap?" If all of the clients are equally persistent in retaining him without delay, upon what principle should he select one or more and reject the rest? Among how many different attorneys should the ten clients be apportioned?* What is the degree of pov-

* The editor suggests, in answer to these queries, that he would draw the line "exactly where professional opinion would say it ought to be drawn in the matter of an attorney's being a witness in his clients' cases. An attorney (he adds) may *occasionally* be a witness for the client whose cause he is advocating, but if he falls into that *habit* it is apt to make unpleasant remark. Judge C. would hardly recommend it as a *practice*." No, he would not, nor tolerate it in a single instance. There may be cases where it is necessary to examine the attorney in reference to some technical step or pro-

erty on the part of the client, that will justify the acceptance of his contingent retainer? These questions suggest their own answers. There can be no compromise between right and wrong. If the practice of receiving contingent fees be disreputable, demoralizing and degrading, as you have insisted, no "highminded" lawyer can descend to it even once, under any circumstances. If "the lawyer who makes this his practice becomes a huckster," even though he is fair and honest in his dealings, how can the attorney be properly characterized who, while professing to regard

---

ceeding in the action, or formal demand made by him, before he could properly institute the suit; but the lawyer should always refuse to be employed in a case where he is expected to be a material witness to the *merits* of the controversy. He can never be permitted to accept such a retainer. It places him directly in the attitude of bargaining for a favorable version of the matter to his client.

A witness ought, as far as possible, to be disinterested and impartial between the parties. If from circumstances beyond his his control, such as relationship or prior pecuniary interest, he is already directly or indirectly concerned in the contest, he is not disqualified; but these facts are important factors in determining the weight of his testimony. But no one has a moral right to deliberately place himself under special obligations to one of the parties, so that he will be interested in coloring his testimony. If one, expecting to be a witness, should receive a consideration directly for such a purpose, it would clearly be a crime. If he should endeavor to hide the real purpose under ostensible and collateral business engagements, the moral aspect of the transaction would not be changed. And this is precisely the position of the lawyer who accepts, under such circumstances, the retainer of one of the parties. A man of honor would resent the first offer retain him in such a cause, as a personal insult, and an improper attempt to influence his testimony. This suggestion, therefore, will not extricate the editor from his "tub."

the practice as dishonorable, avails himself of such a loop-hole of escape as you have furnished him, to take into his net "now and then" "a few" of this class of cases? I reserve the right, if it should become necessary, to depict this creature in his true colors on some future occasion.

You have suggested with great apparent candor that I must "have some instinctive doubt of the propriety of the practice," because I "leave it to the client to make the advance." Let me put you to the test. You profess to think it is right to make a contract for an absolute fee. Would you deem it delicate and proper to suggest to your client that the first thing in order was the amount of your fee? Or if you failed to do so from an instinctive sense of decency, would you regard it as a fair inference that you entertained any doubts of the propriety of such a contact if the client desired it?

E. COUNTRYMAN.

ALBANY, June 21, 1881.

P. S.—Since writing the above, my attention has been called, by a leading lawyer of Western New York, to an editorial in the Albany Law Journal of September 26, 1874. (10 Alb. Law Jour., 193.) Its flavor is so delicious that I cannot forego the pleasure of sending to you a few choice bits as a desert. I quote: "The old statute was part of a system under which lawyers were viewed and treated very much as malefactors. The Legislature and the public seemed to regard them as a class of reprehensible persons, who were not to be paid for their services like other people. If they were permitted to work it was mainly for the public benefit and behoof, like the convicts in our prisons. It was meritorious to restrict their compensation to a meagre pittance. It was even esteemed by many a venial offence to cheat a lawyer out of his pay. Agreements between attorney and client in respect to the *subject matter of the litigation*, were always construed as frauds upon the client. The public were to be protected against these ravening wolves by legislation, and if the costs of a suit could be charged upon the lawyer it was a joke that made godly persons laugh. But when common sense and the Code came in, we tried to change all that. We left lawyers at liberty to make contracts for their compensation *like other persons*. It is notorious that an immense amount of legal business is now transacted in this State by the *most reputable lawyers*, under agreements precisely like that impliedly censured by the court in *Voorhies* v. *Mc-Cartney* (one of your authorities), although seldom, we hope, entered into under the same circumstances. It is an *affectation* at this day to frown upon this mode of doing legal business." "We can see *nothing immoral or impolitic* in such arrangements." "There is a great deal too much of this *sentimental nonsense* in regard to the members of the learned professions. A physician must not advertise ; a clergyman must not care for the amount of his salary ; a lawyer must not have any pecuniary interest in the result of his client's cause.　We had supposed that the sturdy sense of our profession, in this State at least, had weeded out this last idea.　We knew it was legally ex_tinct ; we hoped it was *morally defunct !* "　Does the Law Journal refuse to recognize this authentic " apology ? "

E.　C.

www.ingramcontent.com/pod-product-compliance
Lightning Source LLC
Chambersburg PA
CBHW031419180326
41458CB00002B/437